BIOGRAPHY
A Game

THE
SEAGULL
LIBRARY OF
GERMAN
LITERATURE

MAX FRISCH

BIOGRAPHY
A Game

New Version, 1984

TRANSLATED BY BIRGIT SCHREYER DUARTE

LONDON NEW YORK CALCUTTA

This publication was supported by a grant from the
Goethe-Institut, India.

Seagull Books, 2022

Originally published in German as Max Frisch,
Biografie: Ein Spiel; Neue Fassung 1984
© Suhrkamp Verlag, Frankfurt am Main, 1984

First published in English translation by Seagull Books, 2010
English translation © Birgit Schreyer Duarte, 2010

ISBN   978 1 8030 9 215 7

British Library Cataloguing-in-Publication Data
A catalogue record for this book is available
from the British Library

Typeset by Seagull Books, Calcutta, India
Printed and bound by WordsWorth India, New Delhi, India

DRAMATIS PERSONAE

Hannes Kürmann

Antoinette Stein

Director

Female Assistant

Male Assistant

PART ONE

Centre stage are various pieces of furniture which, under the stage lights, suggest a living room: desk, sofa, easy-chair, musical clock, floor lamp. When the working lights are on, one can see the bare back wall, the backstage installations. Down-stage, left or right, is a director's desk with a small neon light, and two chairs. As the curtain rises: stage lighting; Antoinette is sitting in the easy-chair, waiting, wearing horn-rimmed glasses; Kürmann is standing beside the director's desk, therefore outside the living room scene. Director is also sitting. Female Assistant is sitting with a dossier in front of her.

DIRECTOR. Are the ashtrays there?

ANTOINETTE. No.

DIRECTOR. Why are there no ashtrays?

Enter Male Assistant with ashtrays.

MALE ASSISTANT (M.A.). Sorry!

(*He puts down three ashtrays and steps back.*)

Female Assistant is flipping through the dossier; then she reads out—

FEMALE ASSISTANT (F.A.). 'After the guests had left, she just sat there. What do you do with a strange lady who won't leave, who just stays and sits there in

silence at two o'clock in the morning? It didn't
have to be that way . . .'

Neon light off.

KÜRMANN. It didn't have to be that way.

DIRECTOR. Give me your jacket, Herr Kürmann.

KÜRMANN. Sure.

> *Director puts on Kürmann's jacket.*
> *Gong.*
> *Director enters the scene as Kürmann.*

ANTOINETTE. I'll be leaving soon, too.

> *Silence. Kürmann stands helplessly, then begins
> clearing the bottles and glasses, then the ashtrays, then
> stands helplessly again.*

DIRECTOR. Are you feeling unwell?

ANTOINETTE. On the contrary.

> (*She takes a cigarette.*)

Just one more cigarette.

> (*She waits in vain for a lighter.*)

If I'm not bothering you.

> (*She lights it and smokes.*)

I had a really good time. Some of them were very
nice, I found, very inspiring . . .

> (*Silence.*)

Is there anything left to drink?

> *Director walks over to a small house bar and pours
> some whisky, fumbling awkwardly to emphasize his
> silence but polite, like a host who has no other choice.*

DIRECTOR. Ice?

> (*He hands her the whisky.*)

ANTOINETTE. And yourself?

DIRECTOR. I have to work tomorrow.

ANTOINETTE. What do you do?

The clock strikes two.

DIRECTOR. It's two o'clock.

ANTOINETTE. Are you still expecting someone?

DIRECTOR. On the contrary.

ANTOINETTE. You are tired.

DIRECTOR. Exhausted, yes.

ANTOINETTE. Why don't you sit down?
(*Director remains where he is and says nothing.*)
I can drink faster.
(*Pause.*)
Actually, I just wanted to hear your old musical clock again. Musical clocks have always fascinated me—these figures that always make the same gestures every time it goes off, and each time it's the same song, and yet you're anxious to see it again. Aren't you?
(*She slowly empties her glass.*)

DIRECTOR. Another whisky?

Antoinette puts out her cigarette.

ANTOINETTE. I am leaving now.

DIRECTOR. Do you have a car?

ANTOINETTE. No.

DIRECTOR. May I drive you?

ANTOINETTE. I thought you were tired.

DIRECTOR. Not at all.

ANTOINETTE. Neither am I.
(*She takes another cigarette.*)

Why are you looking at me like that? Do you still have your lighter? Why are you looking at me like that?

Director gives her a light, then goes back to the house bar and pours himself a whisky. He stands with his back to her, glass in hand, not drinking.

DIRECTOR. Did you just say something?

ANTOINETTE. No.

DIRECTOR. Neither did I.
(*Silence. She calmly smokes her cigarette. Director looks at her, then sits down in a chair, crosses his legs and demonstrates that he's waiting. Silence.*)
What do you think of Wittgenstein?

ANTOINETTE. What made you think of Wittgenstein?

DIRECTOR. Just an example.
(*He drinks.*)
After all, we can't just sit here in silence until the sun comes up and the birds start singing.
(*He drinks.*)
What's your opinion on the Krolevsky Case?

ANTOINETTE. Who's Krolevsky?

DIRECTOR. Professor Krolevsky, who was here tonight—Professor Vladimir Krolevsky. What do you think of Marxist-Leninism? I could also ask: how old are you?

ANTOINETTE. Twenty-nine.

DIRECTOR. What do you do, where do you live?

ANTOINETTE. In Paris, at the moment.

DIRECTOR. —and yet I feel no need to know that, to be perfectly honest—not in the least. I'm only asking so that I'm not silent, not impolite.

At two o'clock in the morning. You're forcing me
to display a curiosity that doesn't exist. To be perfectly honest. And even that, you see, I'm only saying because someone is talking in this room at two
o'clock in the morning.
(*He drinks.*)
I know what's going to happen next!

ANTOINETTE. What?

DIRECTOR. The more silent the lady is, the more convinced the man is that he is responsible for her
boredom. And the more I drink, the less comes to
my mind. And the less comes to my mind, the
more openly I will talk, the more personally—only
because we are alone. At two in the morning.
(*He drinks.*)
I know it!
(*He drinks*)
—and meanwhile, you're not even listening to me,
believe me, not at all. You're just smoking in silence
and you're just waiting until I have nothing more
to say other than the mere fact that we're a man
and a woman—

Antoinette puts out her cigarette.

ANTOINETTE. Why don't you call me a cab?

DIRECTOR. You only have to ask for one.

ANTOINETTE. I really am listening to you.

Director stands up.

DIRECTOR. Do you play chess?

ANTOINETTE. No.

DIRECTOR. Then you'll learn tonight.

ANTOINETTE. Why?

(*Director goes out.*)
Why don't you call me a cab?

Director returns with a game of chess.

DIRECTOR. Here—the pawns. They can't move back-
wards. This is a knight. There are also rooks.
Here—these are bishops. One on white, one on
black. This is the queen. She can do whatever she
wants. The king.
(*Pause, until he is finished putting up all the figures.*)
I am not tired, but we won't speak until the sun
comes up and the birds start singing—not a word.
(*She takes her purse and stands up.*)
You can sleep here but it would be better if you
didn't, to be perfectly honest, I would prefer that.
(*She sits down on the sofa to put her lipstick on.
Director is sitting in front of the chess board and
stuffing a pipe, looking at the board.*)
It's your turn.

ANTOINETTE. I have to work tomorrow.

DIRECTOR. You get to be white since you're the guest.
(*He tries to light his pipe.*)
I'm not drunk and neither are you. We both know
what we don't want.
(*He needs a second match.*)
I'm not in love.
(*He needs a third match.*)
You see, I'm already talking quite intimately, and
that's precisely what I didn't want to happen—and
I don't even know your name.

ANTOINETTE. Antoinette.

DIRECTOR. We've only just met today. Please allow me
to call you by your surname.

ANTOINETTE. Stein.

DIRECTOR. Fräulein Stein—

Antoinette puts the lipstick cap back on.

ANTOINETTE. I don't play chess.

DIRECTOR. I will explain it to you turn by turn. You open with the king's pawn. Good. I secure, also with the king's pawn. Now you come out with the knight.
(*She powders her face.*)
Fräulein Stein, I like you.

ANTOINETTE. Why?

DIRECTOR. I don't know, but if we don't play chess now then I know what'll come next. I'll worship you, to everybody's surprise. I'll spoil you. I'm good at that. I'll go to the ends of the earth for you, you were made to be spoiled. I'll believe that I can't live without Antoinette Stein. I'll make it my destiny. For seven years. I'll keep going to the ends of the earth for you until we need two lawyers.

Antoinette closes her compact case.

DIRECTOR. Let's play chess.
(*She stands up.*)
What are you looking for?

ANTOINETTE. My jacket.

Director stands up and hands her the jacket.

DIRECTOR. We will both be grateful, Antoinette, for seven years, if you allow me to call you a cab now.

ANTOINETTE. By all means.

Director goes to the telephone and orders a cab.

DIRECTOR. It'll be here any minute.

ANTOINETTE. Thank you.

DIRECTOR. No, I thank you.
(*Pause, they look at one another.*)
—like two cats. Meow. You must hiss. Hssss. Or I'll hiss.
(*Antoinette stands up and takes out a cigarette.*)
Meow, meow, meow.
(*Antoinette lights the cigarette.*)
You're really good at that: your eyes—when you're smoking and at the same time you're closing your eyes almost completely, those slit eyes—now—excellent.

ANTOINETTE. Hssss.

DIRECTOR. Meow.

ANTOINETTE & DIRECTOR. Meow-ow-owow-ow.
(*They laugh.*)

ANTOINETTE. Let's be serious.
(*Director takes her jacket.*)
What are you doing?
(*Doorbell rings.*)
My cab's here.

DIRECTOR. Let's be serious.
(*He takes off her horn-rimmed glasses.*)

ANTOINETTE. You could at least turn off the light.

Kürmann jumps up from Director's desk.

KÜRMANN. Stop! —Stop . . .
(*Work lights.*)
Can I start again?

DIRECTOR. Please—go ahead.

KÜRMANN. That cat game—that was the mistake. That stupid cat game! And taking off her glasses.

DIRECTOR. That's what you want to change?

KÜRMANN. Definitely.

Director hands the horn-rimmed glasses back to Antoinette.

DIRECTOR. Please.
(*Director goes back to his desk.*)
Herr Kürmann, where would you like to start again?

KÜRMANN. When the clock strikes two.

Neon light on.

F.A. 'Actually, I just wanted to hear your old musical clock again. Musical clocks have always fascinated me—these figures that always make the same gestures every time it goes off—'

Director takes off the jacket and gives it to Kürmann, who puts it on and then enters the scene.

DIRECTOR. Please.

Stage lighting.

Antoinette is sitting in the easy-chair again and Kürmann stands where Director was when the clock struck two.

KÜRMANN. I have to work tomorrow.

ANTOINETTE. What do you do?

KÜRMANN. It's two o'clock.

Director slams his hand on the desk.

DIRECTOR. Where are the clock chimes!

M.A. steps forward.

M.A. Which clock chimes?

DIRECTOR. Two o'clock.

M.A. Why is it two o'clock again?

DIRECTOR. We are going back again.

M.A. I'm sorry.
(*Exits.*)

DIRECTOR. And the jacket!—
(*Kürmann gives the jacket back to Antoinette.*)
That's exactly what Kürmann wants to change! We must avoid him taking off your jacket and you becoming his wife.

ANTOINETTE. I'm sorry.

DIRECTOR. That's the whole point!

Antoinette puts on her jacket.

ANTOINETTE. I see . . .

DIRECTOR. Kürmann doesn't want you to stay—

ANTOINETTE. I see . . .

KÜRMANN. I have to work tomorrow.

ANTOINETTE. What do you do?

The clock strikes two.

KÜRMANN. It's two o'clock.

ANTOINETTE. Are you still expecting someone?

KÜRMANN. On the contrary.

ANTOINETTE. You are tired.

KÜRMANN. Exhausted, yes.

ANTOINETTE. Why don't you sit down?

Pause.

DIRECTOR. Keep going!

Antoinette takes out her compact case.

ANTOINETTE. Is that correct? Or should I rather take a cigarette? If he wants me to leave, then I almost think it's better if I take my compact—

DIRECTOR. As you wish.

Antionette powders her face.

ANTOINETTE. Actually, I just wanted to hear your old musical clock again. Musical clocks have always fascinated me—these figures that always make the same gestures every time it goes off, and each time it's the same song, and yet you're anxious to see it again.

KÜRMANN. I know.

ANTOINETTE. Aren't you?

Kürmann goes to the musical clock and winds it. A cheerful jingle is heard. Kürmann keeps winding the clock barrel until the song is finished.

KÜRMANN. Is there anything else I can offer you?
(*He goes over to the house bar.*)
Unfortunately, there's no more whisky.

ANTOINETTE. That's okay.
(*She takes out a cigarette.*)
What do you think of Wittgenstein?

Kürmann pours himself some whisky.

KÜRMANN. I have to work tomorrow.

ANTOINETTE. What do you do?

Kürmann drinks.

DIRECTOR. Why don't you say it?

ANTOINETTE. What do you do?

KÜRMANN. Behavioural research.
(*He drinks.*)

DIRECTOR. Keep going!

KÜRMANN. Frau Hubalek comes in at eight.

ANTOINETTE. Who's Frau Hubalek?

KÜRMANN. My housekeeper.

DIRECTOR. Stop!
(*Work lights.*)
You can't say that, Herr Kürmann. As soon as you see a young lady in your apartment at two in the morning, you're already thinking of the fact that at eight your housekeeper comes in?!

KÜRMANN. Let's start again!

DIRECTOR. Then you announce that you ran out of whisky—and after you've lied to her, you grab another bottle and pour yourself a whisky!

ANTOINETTE. I didn't even notice that.

KÜRMANN. Let's start again!

DIRECTOR. From the top?

KÜRMANN. Yes, please.

DIRECTOR. As you wish.

KÜRMANN. Why is she not wearing glasses all of a sudden?

DIRECTOR. That is entirely up to the lady—you have no control over that, Herr Kürmann. What you can choose here is your own behaviour. Try to remain casual, never mind the horn-rimmed glasses. And stop thinking, 'I know what's going to happen next.' You come in, whistling away, a man at the top of his career. You've just become Professor—

KÜRMANN. I know.

DIRECTOR. Your friends have thrown a party to celebrate, a surprise party, and you're meeting your wife for the first time—totally casual.

KÜRMANN. Easy to say.

DIRECTOR. Totally casual, totally relaxed.

Kürmann exits.

ANTOINETTE. From the top?

DIRECTOR. If you would.

Neon light off.

ANTOINETTE. Should I wear the horn-rimmed glasses or not?
(*Stage lighting. Voices offstage, laughter, then silence; shortly after, Kürmann enters the room, whistling to himself until he sees the young lady in the easy-chair.*)
I'll be leaving soon, too.

DIRECTOR. Are you feeling unwell?

ANTOINETTE. On the contrary.
(*She takes out a cigarette.*)
Just one more cigarette.
(*She waits in vain for a lighter.*)
If I'm not bothering you.
(*She lights it and smokes.*)
I had a really good time. Some of them were very nice, I found, very inspiring . . .

Kürmann says nothing.

DIRECTOR. Go on!
(*Kürmann goes to the house bar and pours some whisky into a glass.*)
Try not to think of Frau Hubalek now.

Kürmann hands over the whisky.

ANTOINETTE. And yourself?

KÜRMANN. I have to work tomorrow.

ANTOINETTE. What do you do?

Pause.

DIRECTOR. Now you're silent again!

Antoinette puts on her horn-rimmed glasses.

ANTOINETTE. Why are you looking at me like that?

DIRECTOR. The longer you are silent, the more ambiguous the silence becomes—can't you feel that yourself? The more intimately you will have to talk to her later.

ANTOINETTE. Why are you looking at me like that?

The clock strikes two.

KÜRMANN. It's two o'clock.

ANTOINETTE. I am leaving now.

KÜRMANN. Do you have a car?

ANTOINETTE. Yes.

(*She smokes calmly.*)

KÜRMANN. But earlier she said no, she didn't have a car. Now she said yes—so that I can't call her a cab! I won't let her out of this house!

Director enters the scene.

DIRECTOR. May I tell you the mistake you're making right at the very beginning? As soon as you see a young woman in the room, a stranger, you're thinking of a story you already know—am I right? That's why you're so awkward, that's why you don't know what to say—

KÜRMANN. I want her to leave.

DIRECTOR. So that she won't become your wife?

KÜRMANN. Yes!

DIRECTOR. There you have it—you're not acting according to the present but following a memory. That's what this is. You believe you already know the future from your own experience. That's why you always end up with the same story.

KÜRMANN. Why doesn't she leave?

DIRECTOR. She can't.

KÜRMANN. Why not?

DIRECTOR. If she takes her purse now and gets up, then she's guessed what you're thinking—and that'd be embarrassing for you. Why don't you talk about behavioural research? In a comprehensible way? Why do you assume that the young lady wants what you don't want? Any ambiguousness is coming from your part.

KÜRMANN. Hm.

DIRECTOR. You consider yourself a connoisseur of women because you keep making the same mistake towards each one of them!

KÜRMANN. Go on!

DIRECTOR. It's your own fault if she doesn't leave.
(*He returns to his desk.*)
Here we go—

The clock strikes two.

KÜRMANN. It's two o'clock.

Antoinette puts out her cigarette.

ANTOINETTE. Are you still expecting someone?

KÜRMANN. Yes.

DIRECTOR. Good!

KÜRMANN. But not a woman.

DIRECTOR. Very good!

KÜRMANN. I'm expecting an adolescent male . . .

(Antoinette takes her purse.)

I'm expecting an adolescent male.

DIRECTOR. Don't say it twice as if you don't believe it yourself! And don't say 'an adolescent male'—that's what people say when they don't really know what they're trying to say. Say, 'A student who plays chess.' 'A young and highly talented person.' 'A prodigy I'm supporting.' Just talk about his genius. That'll do.

KÜRMANN. Was there a knock on the door?

ANTOINETTE. I didn't hear anything.

KÜRMANN. Hopefully, nothing's happened to him.

DIRECTOR. Good.

KÜRMANN. Every night I'm so afraid that—

Antoinette crushes an empty cigarette pack.

ANTOINETTE. Now I have no cigarettes left!

Kürmann lights his pipe.

KÜRMANN. A student . . . highly talented. . . . Unfortunately, he's compulsively jealous. If he came here now and found a woman in my apartment at two in the morning, he'd be capable of shooting her.

DIRECTOR. Don't exaggerate, though.

KÜRMANN. A Sicilian . . . but blonde, you know, blonde with blue eyes . . . that comes from the Normans . . . yet his lips are Greek . . . A musical

prodigy, by the way . . . a great-grandson of
Pirandello, by the way.

DIRECTOR. Now you're talking too much.

ANTOINETTE. Hopefully, nothing's happened to him.

Kürmann is smoking his pipe hurriedly.

ANTOINETTE. Maybe you want to make a call?

KÜRMANN. Where?

ANTOINETTE. Do you have any cigarettes left?

KÜRMANN. Take my pipe.
(*He wipes it and gives it to her.*)

ANTOINETTE. And yourself?

KÜRMANN. It's a light tobacco, 'Early Morning Pipe'.
(*She puts the pipe in her mouth.*)
What I just said is between you and me, Fräulein
Stein. You see, the University doesn't know about
any of this.
(*She coughs.*)
You need to inhale—slowly and regularly.
(*He takes the pipe and shows her how to smoke it.*)
Like this. You see? Just like this.
(*He wipes it and gives it back.*)
Slowly and regularly.

Antoinette smokes slowly and regularly.

ANTOINETTE. Are you able to think at the same time?

KÜRMANN. Make sure it doesn't get too hot.

Antoinette smokes slowly and regularly.

ANTOINETTE. All my friends, I mean my real friends,
they live the way you live. (*Exhaling.*) Almost all of
them. (*Exhaling.*) Practically all of them. (*Exhaling.*)
All the other men, you know, are terrible. Sooner

or later, they'll nearly always misunderstand a woman.

KÜRMANN. Is that right?

ANTOINETTE. Oh yes.

Antoinette coughs.

KÜRMANN. Slowly and regularly.

Antoinette smokes slowly and regularly.

ANTOINETTE. If it wasn't for Claude-Philippe, for instance!

KÜRMANN. Who's Claude-Philippe?

ANTOINETTE. My friend in Paris. I live with him. A true friend. I can do whatever I want, come and go whenever I want. He always understands.

KÜRMANN. What else does he do?

ANTOINETTE. He's a dancer.

KÜRMANN. Ah.

ANTOINETTE. All the other men, almost all of them, are boring, even the smart ones. As soon as we're alone, they become affectionate or nervous— suddenly, they can't think of anything else other than the fact that I'm a young woman. Hardly anyone asks what I do for a living—and, when I speak of my work, they only look at my lips. It's horrible! As soon as you're alone with them at two in the morning, they think God knows what—you wouldn't imagine! Meanwhile they're afraid, especially the intellectual ones.
(*She sucks on her pipe.*)
Now it's out.

Kürmann takes the pipe to re-light it.

ANTOINETTE. I am glad I met you, you know, very glad.

KÜRMANN. How come?

ANTOINETTE. I don't have any brothers.
(*She stands up.*)

KÜRMANN. Do you want to leave already?

ANTOINETTE. I have to work tomorrow.

KÜRMANN. What do you do?

ANTOINETTE. I'm a translator. I'm from Alsace. Claude-Philippe's being an incredible help. He doesn't speak German but he has a fine sense for it—unbelievable . . .
(*Pause.*)
Hopefully nothing has happened to him, really.

Kürmann helps her into her jacket.

KÜRMANN. If you ever need anything—

ANTOINETTE. You're very kind.

Kürmann takes her hand.

DIRECTOR. Stop! Why're you taking her hands now?— instead of standing there like a brother, hands in your pockets, fine sense and so on, but hands in your pockets, like a brother before his sister.
(*Kürmann tries it.*)
But more casually!
(*He walks into the scene, takes the jacket once again, steps in as Kürmann to show him how to do it.*)
What was your last sentence?

ANTOINETTE. 'I don't have any brothers.'

DIRECTOR. And your reply was?

KÜRMANN. That was not her last sentence.

F.A. 'All my friends, I mean my real friends that are there for a lifetime, are homosexuals. Almost all of them. Actually all of them.'

DIRECTOR. And your reply was?

KÜRMANN. That's wrong—

ANTOINETTE. 'If it wasn't for Claude-Philippe—'

KÜRMANN. That's fine but she said that earlier—that she has a real friend in Paris, who is a dancer. To that I can't say, 'If you ever need anything.'

DIRECTOR. What was his last sentence?

F.A. 'If you ever need anything.'

DIRECTOR. And your reply was?

ANTOINETTE. 'You're very kind.'

Director hands her the jacket.

KÜRMANN. I'm sorry, but this is wrong. If I'm giving her the jacket, how can I have my hands in my pockets now that she's getting affectionate? You should try that.

Director takes the jacket back.

DIRECTOR. All right, then—

ANTOINETTE. I am glad that I met you, you know, very glad.

DIRECTOR. Go on.

ANTOINETTE. I don't have any brothers.

DIRECTOR. So we've heard.

KÜRMANN. What do you do?

ANTOINETTE. I'm a translator.

DIRECTOR. No—

ANTOINETTE. I'm from Alsace.

DIRECTOR. —your last sentence before the jacket!

ANTOINETTE. 'He doesn't speak German but he's got a fine sense for it—'

DIRECTOR. And your reply was?

KÜRMANN. Nothing. I'm wondering how a French who doesn't speak German can have a fine sense for it. I admit that I could have asked her at this point: 'What do you translate?'

ANTOINETTE. Adorno.

DIRECTOR. But you didn't say that!

ANTOINETTE. Because he didn't ask.

KÜRMANN. Because I want her to leave. I'm asking myself: 'Why doesn't she stay in Paris?' But that's none of my business. —Pause! And since I am making a pause, she thinks I'm thinking about my young Sicilian.

ANTOINETTE. I really hope nothing has happened to him.

DIRECTOR. Keep going!

KÜRMANN. You want to leave already?

ANTOINETTE. I have to work tomorrow.

KÜRMANN. What do you do.

ANTOINETTE. I'm a translator.

DIRECTOR. Guys—!

ANTOINETTE. 'I'm from Alsace.'

Director lowers the jacket.

DIRECTOR. —I'd like to hear the last sentence before Kürmann hands over the jacket and makes the mistake of taking both her hands.

KÜRMANN. Why is that a mistake?

DIRECTOR. The way you grip her hands will reveal you.

ANTOINETTE. All the other men, you know, are terrible. Sooner or later, they'll nearly always misunderstand a woman.

KÜRMANN. Is that right?

ANTOINETTE. Oh yes.

Director hands over the jacket to her.

DIRECTOR. If you ever need anything—

ANTOINETTE. You're very kind.

Director puts his hands in his pockets, then steps out of the scene.

DIRECTOR. Understood? Like brother and sister. Even if she gave you a kiss now, which is possible, don't forget—you are expecting a young Sicilian. Otherwise, she wouldn't give you the kiss. She's relieved that you're not an ordinary man, Herr Kürmann, not even when you're alone with her.

KÜRMANN. Understood.

DIRECTOR. Give him the jacket again.
(*Kürmann takes back the jacket.*)
So—

Antoinette takes iout a cigarette.

ANTOINETTE. So there were still some cigarettes left, after all.
(*Kürmann gives her a light.*)
Why am I not staying in Paris? I'd like to open a small publishing house, one of my own, where I can do whatever I want. That's why I'm here. And even if the publishing thing doesn't work out, I'll do something else.

(*She smokes.*)
Something of my own. Ideally, I'd like to run a little gallery—

DIRECTOR. You hear that?

KÜRMANN. Why didn't she mention this before?

DIRECTOR. She wants her own life—she's not looking for a man who thinks she can't live without him, who'll go out and buy a gun if he ever finds out one day that she *can* live without him.

ANTOINETTE. In case you want to know—a young man drove me here, a man much younger than Kürmann, an architect who wants to go to Brazil with me.
(*She laughs.*)
What would I do in Brazil?
(*She smokes.*)
That's why I've stayed here for so long because I am afraid he'll be waiting for me downstairs.

KÜRMANN. How could I have known that?

ANTOINETTE. That's why I wanted a cab—in case he's standing by my car, waiting for me.
(*She smokes.*)
I don't want a scene.
(*She steps on the cigarette.*)
Can I have my jacket now?

Kürmann stands, motionless.

DIRECTOR. What are you thinking about?

KÜRMANN. Adorno.

DIRECTOR. Now it's too late, now you know what you could have been talking about with the young lady—Hegel, Schönberg, Kierkegaard, Beckett—

ANTOINETTE. Adorno—

DIRECTOR. Why don't you give her the jacket?

Kürmann gives her the jacket.

KÜRMANN. If I can ever be of any help . . .

ANTOINETTE. You're very kind.

Kürmann puts his hands in his pockets.

KÜRMANN. What kind of car do you drive?

DIRECTOR. Good.

KÜRMANN. Don't forget your purse.

DIRECTOR. If you make no more mistakes now—in the elevator—then you've made it—a biography without Antoinette!

Kürmann switches off the ceiling light.

KÜRMANN. I'll take you to your car.
(*Antoinette sits down.*)
Why is she so pale all of a sudden?

DIRECTOR. That's the pipe.

Antoinette lies down on the easy-chair, eyes closed. Her purse has fallen to the floor.

KÜRMANN. I don't believe her.

Director steps into the scene to feel her pulse, while Kürmann stands at a distance and stuffs his pipe.

DIRECTOR. She's really had a little collapse—you and your 'Early Morning Pipe'! Stop saying, 'I know what's going to happen next.' Her forehead's ice cold.
(*Kürmann lights his pipe.*)

Do you really have to smoke now?—instead of opening a window?! Your being boorish, you know that, you're acting like a barbarian!

KÜRMANN. Better now than seven years later.

DIRECTOR. As you wish.

(*Antoinette gets up.*)

There's no way she can drive now.

ANTOINETTE. I need to go home . . .

DIRECTOR. Can't you see that?

ANTOINETTE. I need to lie down . . .

DIRECTOR. You're risking a life here.

(*Antoinette takes off her jacket.*)

Aren't you going to get a glass of cold water at least—your guest is dizzy.

Kürmann exits.

ANTOINETTE. Please excuse me . . .

(*She opens her dress. She needs to lie down so as not to faint. When Kürmann comes back with a glass of water, she is lying on the sofa.*)

Please excuse me . . .

KÜRMANN. Drink.

ANTOINETTE. That's never happened to me before—so suddenly—such dizziness.

KÜRMANN. Should I call a doctor?

ANTOINETTE. Don't look at me . . .

(*Pause.*)

I'm embarrassed.

DIRECTOR. She'll catch a cold.

KÜRMANN. I know what's going to happen next—

DIRECTOR. Don't you want to get a blanket?

KÜRMANN. —get a blanket and then I'll take my hand-
kerchief and dry her forehead, her temples, her forehead, her eyelids. I know I'll make a good Samaritan.
I'll make her coffee, I'll stay awake all night, I'll be
silent and stay awake all night. I'll take her shoes off
so she'll feel more comfortable and then, finally, it'll
be, 'Would you at least switch off the light!'
(*Pause.*)
You don't have to be embarrassed, Antoinette, these
things happen, Antoinette, you don't have to be
embarrassed.
(*He takes off her shoes.*)

ANTOINETTE. What are you doing?

KÜRMANN. You'll feel more comfortable.
(*He puts the shoes on the carpet.*)

ANTOINETTE. Would you at least switch off the light!

Darkness.

KÜRMANN. Stop! Who just turned off the light? Stop!

Work lights.

DIRECTOR. You don't want to continue?

KÜRMANN. No!

DIRECTOR. Why are you yelling at me—was it I who
gave her the pipe? . . . Professor Kürmann, you said
that if you could ever start over with your life, then
you'd know exactly what you'd want to do better—

KÜRMANN. Indeed!

DIRECTOR. In terms of Antoinette, for example!

KÜRMANN. I don't want her to stay!

DIRECTOR. We know that.

KÜRMANN. I don't want her to become my wife—

DIRECTOR. Then why do you give her the pipe?

Kürmann is silent.

ANTOINETTE. Where are my shoes?
(*Kürmann gives her the shoes.*)
He's absolutely right, it doesn't have to be this way.
I wasn't in love that night either—

KÜRMANN. Then why did you stay?!

ANTOINETTE. —nor the next morning.
(*She straightens her dress.*)
Our marriage didn't have to be.

Director turns on the neon light.

DIRECTOR. Where, Kürmann, would you like to start
again in order to change your biography?

KÜRMANN. Earlier!

DIRECTOR. When?

KÜRMANN. Before that night!

Director flips through the dossier.

DIRECTOR. Before that night . . .

Kürmann also looks at the dossier.

KÜRMANN. Before I become a professor. Before this
group of people throw me a surprise party. Before I
saw Antoinette Stein for the first time.

Antoinette takes her jacket.

ANTOINETTE. Goodbye, Hannes!
(*Exit.*)

KÜRMANN. A superfluous episode.

DIRECTOR. Choose a different one!

KÜRMANN. She wasn't in love at all . . .

DIRECTOR. That we heard.

KÜRMANN. Not even the next morning!
(*He takes the whisky bottle.*)
I was.
(*He fills his glass.*)

DIRECTOR. You have permission to start again,
wherever you please, and to make choices again—
(*Kürmann empties his glass.*)
You're drinking too much.

KÜRMANN. Since she's become my wife, yes.

DIRECTOR. You're forty-nine—

KÜRMANN. I'm turning fifty.

DIRECTOR. Your biography, Professor, is quite impres-
sive, all in all. You're a renowned scientist. The
Kürmann Reflex—a term today's behavioural
research can no longer do without. Your name
shows up in countless footnotes. Actually, the only
thing missing is a call to the United States.

KÜRMANN. Biography!
(*He stares into his empty glass.*)
I refuse to believe that our biographies, mine or
yours, or anyone's, couldn't end differently.
Completely differently. I only need to act differently
one single time—I won't become a professor but
end up in prison, for instance, for three years, then
I'll emigrate to Canada, for instance, or Australia,
and I'll have a biography without Antoinette Stein.

DIRECTOR. As you wish.

KÜRMANN. —and anyway, what about the power of
chance?!
(*Pause. Kürmann kicks against the desk.*)

DIRECTOR. What do you mean by that?

KÜRMANN. Biography!!

(*He pushes the easy-chair over with his foot.*)

I can't stand this furniture any more—

DIRECTOR. Would you like your puberty again?

(*He turns to F.A.*)

When did Herr Kürmann do his habilitation?

F.A. Habilitation?

DIRECTOR. When did he become a professor?

F.A. flips through the dossier.

KÜRMANN. Just once in my life, when I was seventeen, I was sitting on a bike—I remember it very well— before a thunderstorm which never came, streaks of lightning, dust flying high into the air, the smell of holly and tar—just once in my life I had an insight. A true revelation, I know it. I understood some- thing—but what? I can't think of it again, I'm too stupid. Stupid! That's the only thing I'd wish for if I could start again: a different intelligence.

DIRECTOR. You're misunderstanding the rules of our game. You have the permission to make choices again, but with the intelligence you have now. That is a given. You can use it any way you like—to pre- vent errors or to justify them. As you wish. You can specialize it in order to emphasize it—as a special- ist's intelligence. Or as a political intelligence. You can also corrupt it—through a statement of faith or through alcohol. As you wish. But you cannot change its dimensions or its potential, its value. You understand? That is a given.

Antoinette appears in her coat.

KÜRMANN. What does she want now?

ANTOINETTE. My purse.

KÜRMANN. What's that?

ANTOINETTE. I forgot my purse.

KÜRMANN. I said explicitly: We begin again before my wife entered this house for the first time! —So she cannot have forgotten her purse here.
(*Antoinette is searching for her purse.*)
Did you not understand?

Antoinette takes her purse from the sofa.

ANTOINETTE. Found it!
(*She steps out of the scene.*)

DIRECTOR. Well, then, Herr Kürmann—

Kürmann stuffs his pipe.

KÜRMANN. When did I move into this place?

DIRECTOR. As a bachelor.

KÜRMANN. I don't want to move in here!
(*He lights his pipe and smokes.*)

DIRECTOR. When did Herr Kürmann move into this place?

F. A. flips through the dossier.

KÜRMANN. Let's start even earlier—

DIRECTOR. As you wish.

KÜRMANN. Before I moved in here.

DIRECTOR. As you wish.

KÜRMANN. I want to never have seen this furniture!

Director takes the dossier.

M.A. Away with the furniture?

DIRECTOR. Please.

M.A. Easy to say!

DIRECTOR. Herr Kürmann wants to never have seen it.

Kürmann stands and smokes his pipe, Director stands and flips through the dossier while M. A. comes back with white sheets which he drapes overs all the furniture. F.A. helps him.

M.A. There you go!

Kürmann looks at the changed set.

KÜRMANN. Like a winter landscape . . .

Director points at the dossier.

DIRECTOR. Would you like your high-school days again?

Remaining are the work lights—the neon light is turned off at the desk—and one spot light: into its white circle enters M.A., wearing a woollen hat covered with snow, playing a ten-year-old schoolboy who is forming a snowball.

M.A. 'Kürmännchen
won't hit me,
Kürmännchen
Cheese face!'

DIRECTOR. You remember the little Snot?

KÜRMANN. His name is not Snot—

DIRECTOR. That's right. His name's Snotler but you call him Snot because he won't use a Kleenex.

M.A. 'Cheese face,
Kürmännchen
Cheese face!'

KÜRMANN. Stop that.

M.A. 'Kürmännchen
won't hit me.'

DIRECTOR. The kids are teasing you because that day, in the gym hall, you said you'd become a professor one day, a real professor.

M.A. 'Cheese face,
    Cheese face!'

DIRECTOR. You know what happened then?

KÜRMANN. Yes.

M.A. 'Kürmännchen
    Cheese face.'

KÜRMANN. Stop it!

M.A. 'Kürmännchen
    slow pace.'
    (*He throws his snowball.*)

Antoinette steps forward.

ANTOINETTE. Hannes, what did you do?

Neon light on.

DIRECTOR. The snowball fight—when the boy lost his left eye—are you regretting it?

ANTOINETTE. You never told me about that.

DIRECTOR. When was that?

F.A. flips though the dossier.

M.A. 'Won't hit me,
    Cheese face,
    won't hit me.'

DIRECTOR. That's enough.

F.A. points at the dossier.

F.A. Forty years ago.

Neon light off.

DIRECTOR. Would you like to start here again?

Kürmann is thinking about it.

KÜRMANN. That would mean—

DIRECTOR. High school again, graduation again.

KÜRMANN. Puberty again.

DIRECTOR. That as well.

KÜRMANN. All this again?
   (*He steps up to Director's desk.*)
   May I see the dossier?

DIRECTOR. Of course.

   M.A. clears his throat.

DIRECTOR. One moment, please. Herr Kürmann is not
   sure yet whether or not he wants to repeat all this
   just to save little Snot's left eye—

   Kürmann flips through the dossier.

KÜRMANN. When was the story with Helen?

F.A. The mulatto woman?

KÜRMANN. When was that?

F.A. Earlier.

M.A. In America.

KÜRMANN. I know that.

F.A. You mean that one semester in Berkeley?

KÜRMANN. I was a student.
   Why did I come back to Europe?
   (*He looks at Director.*)
   Why didn't I stay in California?

   Director is holding the dossier.

DIRECTOR. You were in love, that's right, you wanted
   to stay with Helen.

F.A. (*American accent [originally in English]*). Hannes, what's the matter with you?

DIRECTOR. She was a mulatto woman. And from her you learned how to make love. A whole semester long.

F.A. (*American accent*). You're going to leave me?

DIRECTOR. You didn't want to leave the girl, that's right, but you flew back to Europe because your mother was dying—

KÜRMANN. Helen!

DIRECTOR. Would you like to make a different choice here?

KÜRMANN. Helen!

DIRECTOR. You're hesitating . . .
(*Pause.*)
Back then, Herr Kürmann, you chose to leave Helen in order to see your dying mother once again.

KÜRMANN (*German accent*). My mother is dying, I have to go.

DIRECTOR. What did Helen say to that?

F.A. (*American accent*). You're a liar, Hannes.

DIRECTOR. What else did she say?

F.A. (*American accent*). Fuck you!

DIRECTOR. And what did your dying mother say?

KÜRMANN. I must always wear warm socks, I mustn't drink, I must get married and always wear warm socks . . .

F.A. (*American accent*). Fuck you!
(*She steps out of the spot light.*)

DIRECTOR. Your father was a baker.

KÜRMANN. I know that.

DIRECTOR. Would you like to see your father again?
(*A fourth spot light: into its grey glow enters M.A., wearing a crooked hat and pushing a bicycle.*)
Your father was an alcoholic.

KÜRMANN. I know that.

DIRECTOR. For your seventeenth birthday, your father shows up with a bicycle. It's new and shiny, the spokes, the handle bar, everything is shiny, it has a front light which is also shiny, it has four gears and a bell—
(*M.A. rings the bell.*)
An English bicycle.
(*M.A. rings the bell.*)
Do you remember the bell?
(*M.A. rings the bell.*)
It was the fulfilment of all your dreams. According to the dossier. He probably had to borrow the money to buy it. An experience you never had again—all your dreams coming true.

KÜRMANN. No.

DIRECTOR. Would you like the bicycle again?

M.A. Hannes—

DIRECTOR. What a lovely father!

M.A. Why won't he take it?

DIRECTOR. Then he'd be seventeen again—

Kürmann looks around.

KÜRMANN. Where is Helen?

DIRECTOR. If you'd like the English bicycle again, Herr Kürmann, as the fulfilment of all your dreams, then

you'd be seventeen years old and there'd be no
Helen in sight.

M.A. What about me?

(*He rings the bell.*)

DIRECTOR. Is it here that you want to start over?
(*M.A. rings the bell.*)
Herr Kürmann has to think about it.

M.A. swears incomprehensibly.

KÜRMANN. I cannot change the fact that he's an alcoholic. A gentle but hopeless alcoholic. What should
I do? It can't be helped that one night or another
he will fall over the staircase. That in the morning,
instead of fresh bread, they'll find his dead body in
the baking house.

M.A. What's he saying?

KÜRMANN. Thanks for the bicycle.

Director flips through the dossier.

DIRECTOR. So this remains as it is?

KÜRMANN. Yes.

DIRECTOR. Therefore the snowball fight as well?

KÜRMANN. Yes.

DIRECTOR. And the eye remains lost . . .

*Kürmann sits down on the covered sofa while Director
remains standing, flipping through the dossier.*

M.A. The sofa, Herr Kürmann, is not here.

KÜRMANN. I know!

M.A. Then why are you sitting on it—

Church bells.

KÜRMANN. What's with the church bells?

DIRECTOR. Maybe you'd like to make a different choice here?

(Kürmann, who had put his face into his hands, now looks up slowly and sees F.A. in a wedding dress, bridal bouquet in her hand and a bridal expression on her face.)

Guggenbuhl, Brigitte, twenty-one, blonde with freckles, only daughter of a pharmacist—you remember? According to the dossier, you knew on the day of the church ceremony that the marriage was a mistake.

Kürmann stands up.

F.A. Hannes! . . .

The church bells stop.

DIRECTOR. Is it here that you'd like to make a different choice?

Kürmann tries to stuff a pipe.

F.A. Why don't you say something?

KÜRMANN. How well I remember it.

DIRECTOR. Perhaps Brigitte also knows that this marriage is a mistake, and is only waiting for you to say it. You as the male! Before you find yourself standing in front of her coffin. Why don't you say it? She'll break down and sob—perhaps. Obviously, it'll come as a shock if you still say no at this point.
(The organ starts to play.)
Herr Kürmann, we are waiting.
(The organ stops.)
Herr Kürmann, the choice is yours again.
(M.A. appears as a priest.)
Herr Kürmann, we are ready.

The organ starts again.

KÜRMANN. I can hear the organ, oh yes.

DIRECTOR. Brigitte loves you.

KÜRMANN. So she thinks, oh yes.

DIRECTOR. She is happy.

KÜRMANN. And that's enough for her, oh yes.
(*He puts the pipe in his mouth, notices that he doesn't have any matches, takes it out of his mouth and puts it back into his pocket.*)

DIRECTOR. What would you like to say?

KÜRMANN. Nothing.

DIRECTOR. Why did you get married?

KÜRMANN. To forget about Helen.

DIRECTOR. And that didn't work?

KÜRMANN. I used her to forget about Helen, and she used me to have a baby, and that's the truth.

The organ stops.

DIRECTOR. Why don't you tell the girl?

Kürmann shakes his head.

F.A. Hannes?

DIRECTOR. Perhaps that would save her life—

F.A. Hannes?

Director reads from the dossier—

DIRECTOR. 'This morning, in a debate with Brigitte who's always willing to forgive me, I said, "Then why don't you hang yourself?!" When I returned from the Institute in the afternoon, she had done it, and now she is lying here in this coffin.'
(*Kürmann is silent.*)

So that remains as it is?

KÜRMANN. I got accustomed to my guilt.

(F.A and M.A. take off their costumes and go over to Director's desk. Kürmann stands alone. Suddenly, he laughs out angrily—)

'The choice is yours again!'

DIRECTOR. *(to F.A.).* Why did Brigitte hang herself?

F.A. takes the dossier.

KÜRMANN. If I hadn't married her, perhaps, she wouldn't have committed suicide, perhaps, and I wouldn't be guilty—yes, perhaps, yes—yes!

DIRECTOR. Why are you yelling?

KÜRMANN. And what about our child?

(He takes out the pipe again.)

A child, once it's born, can't be simply thought away from this world, a child that lives, that goes to school . . . Easy to say, 'The choice is yours again!' —A child is a child.

DIRECTOR. I see.

(Kürmann puts the pipe in his mouth.)

Again, Herr Kürmann has no matches.

(M.A. brings matches.)

So the child is supposed to stay . . .

(Kürmann lights the pipe and smokes.)

How old is this child?

KÜRMANN. Thirteen.

DIRECTOR. Boy or girl?

KÜRMANN. He doesn't live with me, that wasn't possible, her family didn't allow it, but it is my child, her child, our child—

(He needs to re-light his pipe.)

I am paying for him.
(*He stands and smokes.*)

DIRECTOR. So, then we keep that. Your child is born,
you don't want to change that. I understand. If you
can start over, then you don't want to go back further than thirteen years.

KÜRMANN. By no means.

DIRECTOR. As you wish.

F.A. points into the dossier—

F.A. The child is fourteen.

DIRECTOR. Correct.

F.A. Here are all the dates.
(*Director studies the dates.*)
Your child, Herr Kürmann, is fourteen!

DIRECTOR. And when does Antoinette show up?

Antoinette is sitting in the background:

ANTOINETTE. That was seven years ago.

DIRECTOR. Is that correct?

KÜRMANN. That is correct.

DIRECTOR. Well, then—

Antoinette steps forward—

ANTOINETTE. May I say something?

KÜRMANN. No!

ANTOINETTE. Hannes—

KÜRMANN. No!

ANTOINETTE. For the sake of your health—

KÜRMANN. No!

DIRECTOR. There is no need to yell, Herr Kürmann.
(*Kürmann is silent.*)

Well then—
(*Kürmann knocks his pipe on his right heel.*)
Why does Herr Kürmann have no ashtray?

M.A. goes to the covered furniture, picks up a white sheet, takes an ashtray and hands it to Kürmann.

KÜRMANN. I wish for the last time for this young lady, later to be my second wife, to not appear before my eyes again.

ANTOINETTE. That's childish!

KÜRMANN. Now that I have permission to start over in order to change my biography—it is not childish but logical—I am starting again before I see Antoinette Stein for the very first time.

Antoinette smiles.

KÜRMANN. May I ask for springtime, seven years ago?

F.A. flips through the dossier.

DIRECTOR. What happened back then?

F.A. Just one second, one second, please—

KÜRMANN. Where were you in the spring, seven years ago?

ANTOINETTE. In Paris.

KÜRMANN. In Paris.

ANTOINETTE. Yes.

KÜRMANN. There you go!
(*He steps towards Director.*)
Can't you make Antoinette Stein understand that she has nothing to come here for, that she can't have lost anything here—no purse and no bracelet and no brush—since Antoinette Stein, as she

admits herself, was in Paris that spring, and had never been to my bachelor apartment?

F.A. That's true.

KÜRMANN. Can you make her understand that?

Director steps closer to Antoinette.

DIRECTOR. Herr Kürmann requests springtime, seven years ago.

ANTOINETTE. As he wishes.

DIRECTOR. He wants never to have met you.

ANTOINETTE. As he wishes.

DIRECTOR. Herr Kürmann has the choice . . .

KÜRMANN. Other people can take care of her purse! (*Antoinette takes her purse and leaves.*) Thank God!

Director laughs.

DIRECTOR. A behavioural researcher who thanks God.

F.A. reads from the dossier—

F.A. 'My academic work is slowly being acknowledged, I should become a professor, they say, Director of the Behavioural Research Institute, assuming that my political orientation—'

Antoinette comes back.

ANTOINETTE. If he has the choice once again, then please tell my husband that he should see a doctor. Today, that is. The earlier the better. Before it is too late again. After the fact, one always says, 'A few years ago it still would have been curable! If only it had been diagnosed.'

KÜRMANN. I will see a doctor.

ANTOINETTE. Suddenly, there is no hope.

KÜRMANN. I promise, Antoinette.

ANTOINETTE. For nine months I took care of him.

KÜRMANN. I will see a doctor!

Antoinette leaves.

DIRECTOR. What, Herr Kürmann, would you like to do differently in that spring, seven years ago, before you first met this charming young lady?

F.A. reads—

F.A. '—assuming that my political orientation won't hinder a professorship.'

Kürmann walks a few steps and then stops—

KÜRMANN. I decline the professorship!

DIRECTOR. Sorry?

KÜRMANN. Let me have the conversation with Krolevsky once again, who was later dismissed from his teaching position.

F.A. Krolevsky?

KÜRMANN. Vladimir Krolevsky.

F.A. Mathematician.

KÜRMANN. Our conversation in my apartment.

DIRECTOR. Please.

M.A. leaves and takes off the white sheets from the furniture. This takes a while since he also folds the sheets. F.A. is occupied with a thermos bottle.

F.A. A cup of coffee?

DIRECTOR. Later . . .

The white sheets are removed. Kürmann deposits the ashtray, which he wasn't able to get rid of all this time, somewhere on a table and takes off his jacket.

M.A. The ashtray goes here.

(He corrects the position of the ashtray and steps away.)

Stage lighting.

DIRECTOR. Herr Kürmann, your apartment is back again!

Kürmann looks around.

KÜRMANN. What's this?

DIRECTOR. Your old musical clock.

KÜRMANN. Away with it!

DIRECTOR. As you wish.

(M.A. takes the musical clock away.)

Any other changes? Just let us know. Perhaps you'd like the desk on the opposite side?

KÜRMANN. As if that would make any difference!

(Sounds of a piano out of tune.)

Is that necessary?

DIRECTOR. That's the ballet school next door, you remember? Unfortunately, they always leave the windows open.

Repetition of the same bars.

KÜRMANN. Every day?

DIRECTOR. Except Sundays and holidays.

KÜRMANN. But that's unbearable!

DIRECTOR. You used to bear it . . .

(Repetition of the same bars.)

Why don't you choose a different apartment?

KÜRMANN. And what will it be there?

DIRECTOR. An electric drill maybe—

KÜRMANN. A kindergarten class—

DIRECTOR. A streetcar—

KÜRMANN. Or an airport runway!

DIRECTOR. Herr Kürmann, the choice is yours.

One can hear a jackhammer.

KÜRMANN. What's that?

DIRECTOR. A different option.

KÜRMANN. A jackhammer.

Again the sounds of the piano, out of tune.

DIRECTOR. The choice is yours . . .
(*Kürmann drops onto the sofa.*)
So you'are staying in this apartment?
(*Kürmann is touching the sofa.*)
That's how it was, Herr Kürmann.

KÜRMANN. That's how it was . . .

DIRECTOR. Are you surprised by your own taste?

F.A. enters the scene as Frau Hubalek, an old house-keeper with a foreign accent who is constantly rubbing her hands.

F.A. A certain Herr—

KÜRMANN. Professor Krolevsky?

F.A. So he says.

KÜRMANN. Let him in please.

F.A. leaves.

DIRECTOR. That was Frau Hubalek.

KÜRMANN. I know.

DIRECTOR. Who has passed away by now too.

M.A. enters the scene as Vladimir Krolevsky. He is bald, wears a black coat and always holds his hat in his hand. His behaviour is Jewish-shy, his voice quiet although he speaks like an authority. Kürmann gets up but they don't shake hands.

KÜRMANN. I believe you were sitting here.
(*M.A. sits down uncomfortably.*)
You certainly know my reasons for never having joined any political party, my fundamental resentment—I don't need to repeat myself.

M.A. No.

KÜRMANN. Do you take a drink?

M.A. I never drink.

Kürmann pours himself some whisky.

KÜRMANN. My dear colleague, I've thought about it some more.

M.A. What have you thought about, Herr Kürmann?

KÜRMANN. Our talk in this apartment, our certain talk one on one, back then—you over there, me here—you don't need to repeat yourself either, Krolevsky, I haven't forgotten! In your eyes, I'm a bourgeois intellectual who sees through the ruling class, partly anyway, with horror at the most or disgust at the least—what they call a non-conformist, but disgust is enough for him. Once in a while I sign an appeal, a petition in favour of something, a protest against something else—as long as having a conscience is still allowed. Aside from that, the non-conformist is working on his bourgeois career.

M.A. Is that what I said?

KÜRMANN. The way you said it was more refined,
  Comrade Krolevsky.

M.A. How so?

KÜRMANN. More objective.

M.A. Namely?

KÜRMANN. Working in the Party, so you said, is the
  only way to change society—to save the world—as
  long as the ends justify the means, so you believe.
  Which is a well-known fact and the very reason
  why I won't join any party.
  (*F.A. enters as Frau Hubalek, with a letter.*)
  Thank you, Frau Hubalek, thank you.
  (*F.A. exits.*)
  Working in the Party, so you say—and at that
  moment the letter from the Committee arrives,
  inquiring whether I would be willing et cetera,
  acknowledging my academic achievements et cetera,
  by the condition that the government et cetera . . .

M.A. Congratulations, dear colleague, congratulations.

KÜRMANN. In my memory you're always smiling, but
  when I see you in person you never are. Just like a
  chess player. You think you know my next step—
  I'll play the conformist and become Director of the
  Behavioural Research Institute!
  (*He puts the letter aside without opening it.*)
  Do you believe, Krolevsky, you as a physicist, do you
  believe that an individual's biography is, after all,
  actually binding, an expression of a necessity—or
  that I might as well have quite a different biography
  by accident, and that the one that we end up with
  one day, this biography with all the dates that we are
  so fed up with, this one is not even necessarily the

most likely one: it is merely one option, one out of many which would be just as possible under the same social and historical conditions, and with the same preconditions of the person? What then, if you look at it this way, can a biography tell us at all? You understand—whether this biography is better or worse is not the question here. I just refuse to give meaning to everything that once happened—just because it happened, just because it became history and is therefore irreversible—I refuse to give it a meaning which it doesn't deserve.

M.A. I understand.

KÜRMANN. You do?

M.A. *Ab esse ad posse valet, a posse ad esse non valet.* But I think you've been trying to say something important—

DIRECTOR. Herr Kürmann, you're talking to Krolevsky. Suddenly, you stop listening to yourself—you look out the window while you're talking and you see the ballet school next door. Suddenly, you're distracted—

KÜRMANN. I don't know this ballet student.

DIRECTOR. But you could get to know her. You have permission to choose once again: perhaps you'd like to have dinner with her some time. If you have dinner with this girl, I imagine that, four months later, when Fräulein Doctor Stein arrives from Paris, your attitude will be entirely different, Herr Kürmann—more casual, more intellectual, more witty. So that, shortly after two in the morning, Fräulein Doctor Stein will pick up her purse and leave—a biography without Antoinette . . .

KÜRMANN. Who do you think I am?! As if this was about chasing after girls! Now that I have the permission, I'd rather have a story with no women at all!

DIRECTOR. As you wish—so, continue!

M.A. *Ab esse ad posse valet, a posse ad esse non valet.* But I think you've been trying to say something important—

Kürmann sits down on the edge of the table.

KÜRMANN. No beating about the bush, Krolevsky— you don't have to answer me—you're a member of the Communist Party—which is unknown to this day—at least a contact person, probably even a leading head. Your field, mathematics, doesn't expose your involvement at all. Your frequent travels, whether to Prague or Paris or Mexico City, are perfectly disguised by conferences in your special field. Of course, you don't drink either, so you don't start talking too much as the night wears on. Assuming the following—one day, it becomes public, and, under some pretext or the other, your further teaching position will have to be suspended, at least under the name of the Faculty of Philosophy, which to us, or to some of us, will obviously and sincerely be an outrage, a suppression of didactic freedom, et cetera. It becomes the Krolevsky Case. I myself, a non-conformist, will compose an appeal: 'Shocked by the recent events at our university . . .', an appeal as concerned as it is thought-through, which will have been a great honour to sign, and which, by the way—of course—won't have any effect whatsoever.

M.A. You're speaking out of experience.

KÜRMANN. Yes, indeed.

M.A. What is it, dear colleague, that you want to tell me?

KÜRMANN. If we could start all over again, then we would all know what to do differently: signatures for, signatures against, protests, rallies and their outcomes: the powerlessness of the intelligentsia, the violence in the name of the constitutional state, and then, ultimately, terror—the proof of the fact that we never took any action after all.
(*He puts the pipe in his mouth.*)
What I need to tell you—
(*He lights the pipe.*)
I am joining the Communist Party.
(*He smokes.*)

M.A. I have to admit, dear colleague, you surprise me. Joining the Communist Party! I hope you're aware of what this means for your academic career?

KÜRMANN. That's why I'm doing it!
(*He laughs.*)

M.A. The Party will consider your application.
(*He stands up, and so does Kürmann.*)

KÜRMANN. Comrade Krolevsky!

They do not shake hands.

M.A. As far as we are concerned, my dear colleague, our social interactions remain the same. Once in a while, a little talk on campus. Once in a while. We will continue to call each other colleagues.
(*He extends his hand formally—*)
Dear colleague!

KÜRMANN. Colleague . . .

M.A. puts his hat on.

M.A. You know that as a member of our Party you will be under surveillance, at least your telephone? And the police will know who your guests are? If you ever have a so-called get-together here, I will not attend it in the future.

KÜRMANN. What do you mean, a get-together?

M.A. After you've become Professor, for instance.

KÜRMANN. That won't happen!

M.A. exits, and he can be seen, once outside the living room, taking off the hat and coat of Vladimir Krolevsky.

DIRECTOR. Good.

Work lights.

KÜRMANN. May I see the dossier?

DIRECTOR. Please.

Kürmann goes to Director's desk.

KÜRMANN. When did I become Professor?

Neon light on.

F.A. In the fall of that year—

KÜRMANN. When exactly?

F.A. In October.

KÜRMANN. Hm.

F.A. And the party took place in November.

KÜRMANN (*laughs*). That won't happen.
    (*He stuffs his pipe.*)
    That's been changed now.
    (*He lights his pipe.*)

F.A. Would you now like a cup of coffee?

DIRECTOR. Later.
  (*Neon light off.*)
  Let's go on!

  M.A., who has now also taken off the bald head of Krolevsky, brings a chair of the kind used in medical practice and puts it outside the living room area, facing upwards.

M.A. Spot light please!
  (*A spot light on the chair.*)
  Okay.
  (*He leaves.*)

KÜRMANN. What's that for?

DIRECTOR. In case you decide to go and see a doctor. The earlier the better. This might perhaps change your biography as well.

KÜRMANN. I feel perfectly well.

DIRECTOR. That's what you always say—
  (*He flips through the dossier.*)
  When did you have these cramps first?

KÜRMANN. Only during the time with Antoinette.

DIRECTOR. Once the doctors know what it is, they always say, 'Earlier on it would have been curable, no big deal, a minor operation—and it would never have become metastases!'
  (*Kürmann is silent, deep in thought.*)
  Suddenly, there is no hope.

  Kürmann puts on his jacket.

KÜRMANN. Antoinette is right.

DIRECTOR. You'll go see a doctor?

KÜRMANN. The earlier the better . . .

Stage lighting.

DIRECTOR. Look!

F.A. enters the scene as Frau Hubalek.

F.A. Doctor Kürmann is not in.
(*M.A. follows her like a police officer.*)
What is it that you want anyway?

M.A. This is the living room?

F.A. Who are you? I am the housekeeper here. May I
ask you who you are, by the way?

M.A. The Professor lives here by himself . . .

F.A. Yes.

M.A. The Professor is a bachelor . . .

F.A. What business is it of yours?

M.A. You are his housekeeper . . .

F.A. Why don't you take off your hat?

M.A. takes a look around.

KÜRMANN. What is this?

DIRECTOR. House search.

KÜRMANN. They won't find anything.

M.A. looks closely at the desk.

F.A. What are you looking for?

M.A. Nice desk . . .

F.A. The Professor doesn't like his papers to be
touched. Do you understand? He can't stand that,
I'm telling you.

M.A. Just checking.

F.A. prevents him from examining the papers.

F.A. He'll yell at me.

M.A. I understand, I understand.

F.A. Well, I have to say that—

M.A. What do you have to say?

F.A. Why did you enter the apartment? Didn't I tell
you that the Professor is not home. One mustn't do
such things, you shouldn't—
(*M.A. opens a drawer.*)
How some people behave nowadays!
(*M.A. closes the drawer.*)
The Professor has nothing to do with drugs.

M.A. takes a newspaper out of the bin.

M.A. This is the paper that he reads?

F.A. And why not?!

M.A. Just asking.

F.A. This is a decent newspaper.

M.A. Why does he throw it in the bin?

F.A. Because he's finished reading it.

M.A. Without opening the tape around it?

F.A. Maybe he already knows what's in it—

M.A. throws the paper back into the bin.

M.A. Frau—

F.A. Hubalek.

M.A. Tell me, Frau Hubalek—

F.A. I already told you that the Professor is not at
home—and I am telling you one last time, it's not
right.

M.A. Calm down, please.

F.A. Where are we here, in the Soviet Union?
(*M.A. shows her his police ID.*)

What sort of crime did the Professor commit?
(*M.A. puts his ID back.*)
I know of nothing.

M.A. Where are you from, Frau Hubalek?

F.A. East Germany.

M.A. East Germany.

F.A. So what?

M.A. So you've got relatives—

F.A. In East Germany—yes, I do.

M.A. In East Germany.

F.A. Why is this the Professor's fault?

M.A. Answer my questions.

F.A. I know of nothing.

M.A. How often do you visit your relatives in East Germany?

F.A. Never.

M.A. That's not a lot.

F.A. It's enough for me.

M.A. You don't travel back and forth?
(*F.A. laughs bitterly.*)
Tell me, Frau—

F.A. Hubalek.

M.A. Doesn't Doctor Kürmann have a library?

F.A. Over there.

Both of them exit the scene; M.A. in front, F.A. behind him. The scene remains empty. Only the sound of the out-of-tune piano is heard.

DIRECTOR. Good.

(*Stage lighting off. Work lights. The sound of the piano continues.*)

Stop!

Silence.

KÜRMANN. House search . . .

DIRECTOR. You see, Herr Kürmann, it works.

KÜRMANN. They won't find anything.

Director points to the chair in the spot light.

DIRECTOR. You need to take off your jacket.

KÜRMANN. Why?

DIRECTOR. I thought you wanted to see a doctor?
(*Kürmann takes off his jacket.*)
Sit down, please.
(*Kürmann sits in the chair.*)
And show me your arm.

Kürmann rolls up his sleeve.

KÜRMANN. How often did I do that?

DIRECTOR. So many times, Kürmann, like all of us!

KÜRMANN. Till there was no hope—

F.A. enters as a nurse.

F.A. The doctor will be here in just a minute.
(*She takes a blood sample.*)
Keep the cotton pressed down on it.
(*She leaves.*)

KÜRMANN. House search.

DIRECTOR. I thought, Herr Kürmann, that was your
intention—so you wouldn't become a professor, so
that this surprise party wouldn't take place when
Antoinette would be sitting in your living room.

KÜRMANN. Where is she at the moment?

DIRECTOR. During the house search?

KÜRMANN. While I'm at the doctor's office.

Neon light on.

DIRECTOR. At this very hour, Fräulein Stein is still in Paris. Today, she is packing her bags to leave Paris—

KÜRMANN. What for?

DIRECTOR. This, Herr Kürmann, you cannot change.

KÜRMANN. Hm.

DIRECTOR. 'Keep the cotton pressed down on it.'

F.A. returns as the nurse.

F.A. The doctor will be here in just a minute!
(*She puts a band-aid on his arm and leaves.*)

KÜRMANN. House search . . .

DIRECTOR. They won't find anything. Still, don't you worry about it, suspicion is suspicion. That's enough, Herr Kürmann, that's enough. You never threw a single stone, but try to convince the police that you'll never stand in their way!

KÜRMANN. You think that's enough?

DIRECTOR. Nowadays—

KÜRMANN. That's comforting.

DIRECTOR. You're under suspicion of wanting to make the world a better place—nobody will suspect that you only want to alter your own biography.

M.A. enters in a doctor's coat.

M.A. It's not that bad.

KÜRMANN. No—?

M.A. Your ECG's fine.
   (*He looks at the film strip.*)
   Wonderful, even.

KÜRMANN. Thank you.

M.A. What I'm not happy with is your urine.

KÜRMANN. Why?

M.A. Do you have personal worries?

KÜRMANN. Not at the moment—

M.A. You can put your jacket back on, Herr Kürmann.

   *F.A. brings the jacket which Kürmann doesn't put on
   however but places on his knee.*

KÜRMANN. Professor, be honest with me.

M.A. I am.

KÜRMANN. I'm asking you.

M.A. Do you feel any pain occasionally?

KÜRMANN. Where?

M.A. That I'm asking you, Herr Kürmann.

KÜRMANN. Once, as a child, I had mumps, once the
   measles, yes, but other than that—headaches, like I
   said, these headaches recently, after drinking too
   much—that happens.

M.A. (*quietly to F.A.*) Tell him I'll be there in a second!
   (*F.A. leaves.*)
   Your bowel movement is all right?

KÜRMANN. Generally, yes.

M.A. What's important is the general.

KÜRMANN. What don't you like about my urine?

M.A. Don't be alarmed—as I said, it's not too bad.
   Nevertheless, you should take it easy, Herr

Kürmann. We already told you last time—one
shouldn't fool around with one's liver.

KÜRMANN. No stress, I know.

M.A. I would add—no pepper, no mustard, no curry,
nothing spicy at all, no escargots à la Bourgogne,
nothing greasy, no *foie gras*, no seafood in any
case—

DIRECTOR. Let me write that down.

Neon light on.

M.A. No stone fruits—apricots, cherries, plums,
peaches. No garlic. Nothing that causes gas.
Cottage cheese any time, cottage cheese as much as
possible.

DIRECTOR. Vegetables?

M.A. No cabbage—

DIRECTOR. Nothing that causes gas.

M.A. No white beans, no beans at all, no onions, et
cetera. If vegetables, then unsalted.

DIRECTOR. Potatoes?

M.A. Millet, semolina, oatmeal.

DIRECTOR. But unsalted.

M.A. And nothing too cold!

DIRECTOR. No spring water?

KÜRMANN. Where would you get that anyway?!

DIRECTOR. When you're hiking—

M.A. No beer.

DIRECTOR. You mean—no cold beer?

M.A. Whisky, vodka, et cetera, gin, sherry, raspberry
schnapps, et cetera, Steinhager, Grappa, et cetera,

cognac, calvados, marc, et cetera—under no circumstances.

DIRECTOR. What about champagne?

M.A. Oh my god!

DIRECTOR. Not even at a wedding?

M.A. The liver knows no weddings.

KÜRMANN. What about ordinary wine?

M.A. Especially no white wine.

DIRECTOR. And red wine?

M.A. No alcohol at all.

KÜRMANN. Then what?

M.A. Milk.

DIRECTOR. Pasteurized?

M.A. By all means.

DIRECTOR. Mineral water?

M.A. But not carbonated.

DIRECTOR. Nothing that causes gas.

M.A. Tea. But no black tea, of course. I recommend camomile, lime tree blossom, rose hip, peppermint and so on. Coffee by no means. Do you like yoghurt?

DIRECTOR. He asked if you liked yoghurt.

M.A. Yoghurt any time.

DIRECTOR. But not too cold!

M.A. Cottage cheese as much as possible, eggs as little as possible, vegetables any time, but unsalted, seafood by no means—

DIRECTOR. We've got that.

M.A. What you can eat is boiled trout.

DIRECTOR. At least, Herr Kürmann, that's better than
nothing.

M.A. Without butter.

DIRECTOR. Lobster?

M.A. Lobster? Oh my god!

DIRECTOR. What about meat?

M.A. Boiled only. Nothing added. No fat. Nothing
roasted, nothing smoked. Boiled or grilled—unsalted.
And no spices, as I said. No sausages, et cetera—

DIRECTOR. Bread?

M.A. Crisp bread.

DIRECTOR. No fresh buns?

M.A. Nothing that causes gas.

DIRECTOR. Cottage cheese as much as possible . . .

F.A. returns.

M.A. I'm coming, yes, just one moment.

F.A. (*turns to Director*). Should I say who's waiting for
him?

DIRECTOR. That's personal—the audience doesn't need
to hear that.

F.A. (*in English*; *accented*). His girlfriend!
(*Director stops her with a gesture.*)
She wants to go surfing—
(*Director repeats the gesture.*)
She's doing the feminist thing . . .

DIRECTOR. This too can mean an emergency.

*F.A. takes off the nurse costume, goes over to Director's
desk, sits down and reaches for the thermos bottle.*

KÜRMANN. Doctor, what else can you recommend?

M.A. Sweating, lots of sweating.

KÜRMANN. How would I do that?

M.A. Hiking, sauna—

(*He extends his hand to Kürmann—*)

It's not too bad, Herr Kürmann, a minor liver swelling—nothing else was found at all. What's important above all is—no agitation, like I said, no stress.

Spot light off, M.A. disappears.

DIRECTOR. Good.

(*Only the work lights remain.*)

You can put your jacket back on.

KÜRMANN. Not a word about cancer?

DIRECTOR. No.

KÜRMANN. Cottage cheese as much as possible!

DIRECTOR. Yes.

KÜRMANN. Not a word about cancer.

A long pause.

DIRECTOR. Herr Kürmann, what are you thinking about?

Kürmann remains seated, his jacket on his knee.
Voices can be heard—voices at a party that is slowly ending—and laughter, loud but incomprehensible.

KÜRMANN. Who are these people?

DIRECTOR. Friends.

KÜRMANN. What do they want?

DIRECTOR. They're celebrating, Herr Kürmann, celebrating.

KÜRMANN. Why?

DIRECTOR. Vladimir Krolevsky is not among them—

KÜRMANN. What's to celebrate?

DIRECTOR. You've become Professor.

Kürmann jumps up.

KÜRMANN. That's impossible.

DIRECTOR. I'm surprised myself.

KÜRMANN. A member of the Communist Party does not become Professor in this country. That's not possible.

DIRECTOR. Not likely.

(Laughter outside.)

Put on your jacket, Herr Kürmann, and show your intoxicated friends where the elevator is.

(Kürmann puts on his jacket.)

That is something I don't have to explain to you, Professor—that no system guarantees the probable for every case—

M.A. enters as a drunken friend in a raincoat.

M.A. Professor—

KÜRMANN. Out!

M.A. —we'll leave you in peace now, Herr Professor.

KÜRMANN. Out!

F.A. enters in a fur coat.

F.A. Hannes—

KÜRMANN. Out! I said, out!

F.A. What's up with him?

KÜRMANN. Out!

F.A. throws her arms around his neck.

F.A. My sweet Herr Professor!

Kürmann slaps her.

M.A. Hannes—really . . .

KÜRMANN. Out!

M.A. My wife will not tolerate such a thing.

KÜRMANN. Out!

M.A. Monika is my wife.

KÜRMANN. I said—out!

F.A. YOU are tolerating this—you!

M.A. Did you hear that, Monika?

KÜRMANN. Out!
   (*He slaps M.A.*)

M.A. And you wanna be a professor—
   (*F.A. in her fur coat cries.*)
   Monika, we're leaving.

KÜRMANN. Please do.

F.A. We won't put up with this!

KÜRMANN. Please don't.

M.A. Professor or not!

KÜRMANN. Out!
   (*He leads them out of the scene.*)

DIRECTOR. Well . . .
   (*Stage lighting.*)
   'After the guests had left, she just sat there. What
   do you do with a strange lady who won't leave,
   who just stays and sits there in silence at two
   o'clock in the morning?'

*Antoinette is sitting in the chair, as she had at the very
beginning.*

F.A. 'It didn't have to be that way.'

Kürmann returns and sees Antoinette.

ANTOINETTE. I'll be leaving soon, too.
(*Kürmann drops onto the sofa.*)
Are you feeling unwell.
(*Kürmann covers his face with his hands.*)
I'll be leaving soon, too.

Pause.

DIRECTOR. Keep going!

Antoinette takes a cigarette out of her purse.

ANTOINETTE. Just one more cigarette.
(*Kürmann looks at her.*)
Don't you have a lighter?

KÜRMANN. No.

ANTOINETTE. Then how do you light your pipe?
(*She uses her own lighter.*)
Actually, I just wanted to hear your old musical
clock again. Musical clocks have always fascinated
me—

Neon light on.

DIRECTOR. The musical clock was cut.

Neon light off.

ANTOINETTE. I had a really good time. Some of them
were very nice, I found, very inspiring . . .
(*She smokes.*)

KÜRMANN. Do you have a car?

ANTOINETTE. Yes.

KÜRMANN. Otherwise I'd have given you a ride home.
(*She smokes.*)
You are from Alsace?

ANTOINETTE. How did you guess?

The clock strikes two.

KÜRMANN. It's two o'clock.

ANTOINETTE. Tired?

KÜRMANN. I have to work tomorrow.

ANTOINETTE. What do you do?

Kürmann gets up and turns his back to her.

KÜRMANN. Behavioural research.
(*He turns and looks at her.*)
At eight o'clock, Frau Hubalek comes in.

ANTOINETTE. Who is Frau Hubalek?

KÜRMANN. My housekeeper—

Director sighs—

DIRECTOR. —and so on and so on!
(*Neon light on.*)
Is there some coffee left?

F.A. fills a paper cup.

ANTOINETTE. Why don't you turn off the light?

Stage lighting off.

DIRECTOR. Let's take a break!

Curtain.

PART TWO

Stage lighting. F.A., as Frau Hubalek, is cleaning up a room. Grumpily. She finds a pair of women's shoes, examines them and puts them on the desk. Kürmann appears in a bathrobe.

KÜRMANN. Frau Hubalek—good day to you—would you be so kind, Frau Hubalek, as to make some breakfast?
(*He opens letters.*)
Two cups.
(*He reads the letters.*)
I asked if you would be kind enough, Frau Hubalek, as to make some breakfast.
(*F.A. as Frau Hubalek exits.*)
I know exactly what you're thinking now. But you're mistaken. You think I'm going to do the same thing over and over again, even if I start over a million times.
(*He reads.*)
Congratulations!—
(*He throws a bunch of letters into the bin.*)
—but you are mistaken. We will not go for a ride to the countryside. We will not get to know each other. It will be our first and last breakfast.

DIRECTOR. As you wish.

KÜRMANN. She won't succeed.

DIRECTOR. In what?

KÜRMANN. We won't become a couple.

DIRECTOR. The choice is still yours.

Kürmann throws some more letters into the bin.

KÜRMANN. Congratulations, congratulations . . .
(*He sees the women's shoes and puts them on the floor.*)
What day of the week is it?

DIRECTOR. Thursday.
(*Neon light on.*)
At eleven o'clock, you have a conference to go to, remember, an important conference which you missed back then because of Miss Antoinette Stein—

Antoinette enters in her evening dress.

ANTOINETTE. I used your toothbrush.

KÜRMANN. Your shoes are here.
(*She takes her shoes and sits down.*)
I forgot to ask you—tea or coffee? Perhaps you prefer coffee.
(*He walks to the door.*)

ANTOINETTE. No thanks.
(*She puts on her shoes.*)
What time is it actually?

KÜRMANN. At eleven, I have a conference—

Antoinette rummages through her purse.

ANTOINETTE. If only I knew where I parked my car. I have the keys! I only know it's in an avenue some-where—

KÜRMANN. There are no avenues around here.

ANTOINETTE. Strange—

KÜRMANN. Maybe you'd like an egg for breakfast?

ANTOINETTE. I'm surprised every time I find my car again.
(*F.A. as Frau Hubalek sets the table. Both remain silent until she has left.*)
Do you know young Stahel?

KÜRMANN. Stahel?

ANTOINETTE. He drove my car. He didn't want to come up here—he's terribly shy. And the thing with the avenue—now I remember, that was before.
(*The clock strikes ten.*)
Ten o'clock?

KÜRMANN. Yes.

ANTOINETTE. Oh my god—
(*She takes her jacket from the sofa.*)

KÜRMANN. You want to leave already?

ANTOINETTE. Ten o'clock!

KÜRMANN. No breakfast?

ANTOINETTE. I've got work too. Oh my god! I need to get changed—I've got an appointment at ten!
(*Kürmann looks at her while she puts on her jacket.*)
Don't be concerned!

KÜRMANN. Why're you laughing?

ANTOINETTE. Male concerns. I don't sleep with a lot of men, but, each time it happens I'm always happy afterwards to be by myself again. Just like you, Professor.
(*She kisses him.*)
Now where did I leave my watch?

KÜRMANN. In the bathroom, I think.
(*Antoinette leaves.*)
That's how it was?

DIRECTOR. Precisely like this.

KÜRMANN. Not a word of meeting again?

DIRECTOR. Not a word.

KÜRMANN. I don't understand—

DIRECTOR. Your memory, Herr Kürmann, has been making things up. Nobody sat down on your left or right knee, no arm on your neck, no kiss that imposed prolonged tenderness. None of that. She has an appointment too.

KÜRMANN. —that's how it was . . .

DIRECTOR. She's neither disappointed nor confused. On the contrary, apparently she did enjoy that night but what's over is over. She doesn't even insist on the intimacy of the nightly form of address.

KÜRMANN. I don't understand—

DIRECTOR. That's how it was, Herr Kürmann.

KÜRMANN. Then why did I miss my conference?
(*F.A. serves breakfast as Frau Hubalek.*)
What's taking her so long?

F.A. She's looking for her watch.

Antoinette returns and puts on her watch.

ANTOINETTE. It's already quarter past ten . . . Today, I want to look at those rooms again. For my gallery. Unfortunately, the house has no elevator—that's the only catch. But the rooms are marvellous. Just what I've been looking for for years. One could build a skylight. That's why I'm meeting this young architect today.

KÜRMANN. Stahel.

ANTOINETTE. And the location is fantastic.

(*She drinks a cup of tea while standing.*)

DIRECTOR. You only need to guide her to the elevator now.

(*Neon light off.*)

No long kiss.

ANTOINETTE. I hope it works out.

KÜRMANN. Yes—

ANTOINETTE. Cross your fingers for me!

Kürmann brings her outside. The out-of-tune piano is heard again. F.A. as Frau Hubalek brings in the buns for the breakfast.

F.A. Do you still need the buns?

DIRECTOR. Maybe he's hungry—

(*Kürmann returns.*)

Is she gone?

KÜRMANN. Yes.

DIRECTOR. That's new.

KÜRMANN. And what now?

DIRECTOR. Biography without Antoinette . . .

(*Kürmann stands, silent.*)

Herr Kürmann, how are you feeling?

(*Kürmann takes a bun and eats.*)

As far as the eleven o'clock conference is concerned, you remember, it is about the election of the new chair. It might be important, for you too, Herr Kürmann, that your colleague Hornacher doesn't win. His attitude is well-known. Oh, old glory of

fraternity! Hornacher as Director will try anything
so that you, Herr Kürmann, don't stay at the
Institute much longer—
(*Kürmann takes another bun.*)
Are you listening?
(*Kürmann stands—thinking and eating.*)
In the first version of your biography, you missed
today's conference because you didn't want to
believe that a woman, after having slept with you,
prefers to be alone as well—you thought you had to
drive into the country with Miss Stein to eat fish
and drink wine and to take an interest in her plans.
And that same morning Hornacher got elected.

KÜRMANN. By a close vote.

DIRECTOR. Back then, you did regret your absence.
(*Kürmann takes a third bun.*)
Director Hornacher couldn't harm you much—in
the first version of your biography—you were not a
member of the Communist Party, after all.
(*Kürmann does not listen.*)
What is it you're thinking about?

Kürmann pours himself some tea.

KÜRMANN. I've underrated Antoinette as a person.

DIRECTOR. Certainly.

KÜRMANN. What is she going to do now?
(*He stands and drinks his tea.*)

DIRECTOR. Don't you worry about that—a woman of
her vitality and intelligence will find her way for
sure, even without you, Herr Kürmann. This is a
woman who knows what she wants.

KÜRMANN. Oh yes.

DIRECTOR. And attractive too.

(*Kürmann drinks his tea.*)

She'll be managing a gallery, 'Gallery Antoinette', or a small publishing house, 'Edition Antoinette', or something else, 'Boutique Antoinette'. And if it doesn't work out, she can go back to Paris any time.

KÜRMANN. Back to her dancer.

DIRECTOR. This morning, she's meeting with some young architect to find out what a skylight will cost. And one day, who knows, she'll have a baby. That'll change her plans again, but that's something that you, Herr Kürmann, don't need to worry about—Antoinette is gone.

(*Kürmann sits down.*)

Worry about your Institute!

(*The clock chimes.*)

It's time for you to get dressed, Herr Kürmann, so you won't miss this conference again. It's half past ten.

Kürmann stands up.

KÜRMANN. Can we go back?

DIRECTOR. Back?

KÜRMANN. I've underrated this woman.

Work lights.

DIRECTOR. Herr Kürmann wishes to go back.

KÜRMANN. Ten o'clock sharp.

DIRECTOR. As you wish.

Director sighs and sits down.

M.A. Is Antoinette still around?

Antoinette reappears.

ANTOINETTE. What's the matter?

DIRECTOR. We need to go back.

ANTOINETTE. Why?

DIRECTOR. Herr Kürmann has underrated you.
(*Stage lighting.*)
So, please—

Antoinette remains standing and drinks tea.

ANTOINETTE. I hope it works.

KÜRMANN. You want to leave already?

ANTOINETTE. Cross your fingers for me!

KÜRMANN. No breakfast?

The clock strikes ten.

DIRECTOR. Stop!
(*Neon light on.*)
This is wrong. 'The clock strikes ten. She takes her
jacket from the sofa to demonstrate that she wants
to leave—'

ANTOINETTE. Yes.

DIRECTOR. So your jacket is placed on the sofa.

ANTOINETTE. That's right.
(*Takes off her jacket.*)
I've got work too. Oh my god! I need to get
changed—I've got an appointment at ten!
(*She puts on her jacket. She doesn't know her lines.*)

F.A. 'I don't sleep with a lot of men—'

ANTOINETTE. I don't sleep with a lot of men, but, each
time it happens I'm always happy afterwards to be
by myself again. Just like you, Professor.

KÜRMANN. I thought you were calling me Hannes—

Antoinette kisses him.

ANTOINETTE. Now where did I leave my watch?

KÜRMANN. In the bathroom, I think.

Antoinette leaves.

DIRECTOR. I can't really see a big difference, Herr Kürmann, to be quite honest. Do you want to have breakfast together or don't you?

F.A. as Frau Hubalek comes in with a tray.

KÜRMANN. Thank you, Frau Hubalek, thank you . . .

F.A. Now we're out of buns!

KÜRMANN. Thank you, Frau Hubalek, thank you . . . (*Antoinette returns and puts on her watch.*) 'Today, I want to look at those rooms again. For my gallery. The location is fantastic. Just what I've been looking for for years. One could build a sky-light—'
Why are you meeting this architect?

ANTOINETTE. Do you know young Stahel? (*Kürmann takes off her glasses.*) What are you doing!

KÜRMANN. I won't let you go.

ANTOINETTE. You have a conference to go to—

KÜRMANN. Hornacher will get elected anyway!

ANTOINETTE. Give me my glasses.

KÜRMANN. Let me make a suggestion—

ANTOINETTE. Seriously, Hannes, I am asking you.

KÜRMANN. I'll miss this conference, forget Hornacher, and you'll forget this young architect with his sky-light. We'll go for a ride into the country.

ANTOINETTE. Where?

KÜRMANN. Anywhere.

ANTOINETTE. Out into nature!

KÜRMANN. A wonderful day.

ANTOINETTE. Hand in hand through the reeds?

KÜRMANN. We don't need to go walking—we'll sit down in a restaurant by the lake, eat fish and have some light wine with it—Fendant.
(*Antoinette smiles.*)
That's my suggestion, Antoinette.

ANTOINETTE. What is Fendant?

KÜRMANN. Miss Stein, I am asking you.

ANTOINETTE. I thought you were calling me Antoinette . . .
(*Kürmann returns her glasses.*)
Thanks.

KÜRMANN. Why are you laughing?

ANTOINETTE. I thought you wanted to get rid of me.

Work lights.

DIRECTOR. So that stays the same now . . .
(*Neon light off.*)
So, back to the first version—lunch at Hotel Schwanen, discussion about astrology and fascism, alone at home at night, message that Hornacher was elected Director—

KÜRMANN. How should I change that?

DIRECTOR. Saturday morning. The second breakfast with Miss Stein, she has to go see her parents over the weekend, Monday at the Institute, evening drinking aperitifs with Miss Stein, both are booked for the night but a phone call after midnight—the skylight is unaffordable.

KÜRMANN. And so on!

DIRECTOR. Wednesday. Antoinette is flying to Paris—

KÜRMANN. That I don't remember.

DIRECTOR. Evening lecture on Behavioural Research and Darwinism, Thursday. Stomach-ache again, weekend together in Paris, Hotel Pont Royal—

KÜRMANN. And so on and so forth!

DIRECTOR. You know what follows now?

KÜRMANN. Travelling.

DIRECTOR. Happiness in Strasbourg, abortion, happiness in London, hepatitis, happiness in Tarasp—

KÜRMANN. Why are you reading this to us?
(*Director keeps flipping through the dossier.*)
What happens one year later?

Director takes a card out of the dossier.

DIRECTOR. 'ANTOINETTE STEIN / HANNES KÜRMANN / WE'RE GETTING MARRIED'
(*Kürmann empties his pipe.*)
So that remains as it is?
(*Kürmann stuffs his pipe.*)
Herr Kürmann, the choice is yours again.

KÜRMANN. Do we have to repeat everything now?
—even what we don't wish to change . . . even the happiness, the intimacy, all that all over again? That won't work.

ANTOINETTE. No.

KÜRMANN. —the joy, the expectation—and anyway, our talks, our joyful talks . . . How can we repeat all this when all the secrets are used up? How would you want to do that? My jokes, her jokes—who could laugh again?

ANTOINETTE. Couldn't we just skip that?

KÜRMANN. Couldn't we just skip that?

DIRECTOR. Why of all things skip the joy?

ANTOINETTE. You try and repeat the joy.

KÜRMANN. You try and repeat the joy once you know what will follow!

Director flips through the dossier—

DIRECTOR. So what is it that you want to change?

Antoinette laughs—

ANTOINETTE. He wants to change my character.

Director points to the dossier—

DIRECTOR. The abortion?
   (*Kürmann and Antoinette look at each other, hesitate, then shake their heads.*)
   Then what?!

KÜRMANN. I know what I'm going to change.
   (*He steps up to Director's desk.*)
   Here.

DIRECTOR. The scene with the slap?

KÜRMANN. Yes.

DIRECTOR. Please.
   (*Kürmann steps back into the scene.*)
   It's nine o'clock in the morning, Frau Kürmann, and you're still not home. Herr Kürmann doesn't know where you've been since last night—he's waiting for you.
   (*Antoinette steps out of the scene.*)
   Continue!
   (*Stage lighting.*)

You had a sleepless night, you don't know where
Antoinette is . . .
(*Kürmann lights his pipe.*)
You have no idea.
(*The sound of a harmonium being played next door.*)

KÜRMANN. What's that supposed to be?

DIRECTOR. A harmonium.

KÜRMANN. Why?

DIRECTOR. You remember—the ballet school next
door went under? A religious sect is renting the
house now—you can't change that, Herr
Kürmann—and, unfortunately, they always leave
the window open.
(*The harmonium and Hallelujah.*)
If you can't stand it, why don't you look for a different apartment?

F.A. appears as Frau Hubalek.

F.A. There is a gentleman who wishes to talk to you.
(*She hands him a business card and leaves.*)

KÜRMANN. Hornacher?

DIRECTOR. That's new.

KÜRMANN. What does Hornacher want from me?

DIRECTOR. You've become a member of the
Communist Party in order to change your biography, and it has changed, Herr Kürmann—you are
now unacceptable as a professor.

M.A. enters as Director Hornacher.

KÜRMANN. I understand, Director, I understand.
(*He points to a chair.*)

M.A. Thank you, dear colleague.

(He does not sit down.)
I apologize for interrupting your breakfast but I felt
it was not proper to speak before the Senate in this
affair before I made some inquiries with yourself.

KÜRMANN. Director, I am a member of the
Communist Party. That's true. I admit my affilia-
tions to Marxist-Leninism and would like to ask the
Senate to draw their consequences.

M.A. puts his hat on.

DIRECTOR. Wait!

M.A. A clear answer.

DIRECTOR. Perhaps, Herr Kürmann, after having heard
himself, wants to reply differently. Perhaps his
answer now seems too simple to him.

M.A. takes his hat off again.

KÜRMANN. Director—

M.A. I am listening.

KÜRMANN. I do not believe in Marxist-Leninism.
Which does not mean, of course, that the Russian
Revolution was superfluous. I don't believe in
Marxist-Leninism as a saving doctrine for eternity
—that's what I meant to say. On the other hand, I
don't believe in your doctrine of the free entrepre-
neur either. Even less so. To be quite frank, I deny
the Western civilization any moral right for a cru-
sade *(To Director)* That's enough, I believe.

M.A. So do I.

KÜRMANN. And yet, this answer is not true either.

M.A. puts his hat on.

DIRECTOR. Wait!

KÜRMANN. What am I supposed to explain to this shit-head?!

DIRECTOR. Take off your hat again.

M.A. takes off his hat again.

KÜRMANN. Should I tell him what I know about his past—he committed perjury in order to make his academic career, that is proven, but that doesn't bother our Senate—
(*He laughs, then his manner becomes official again.*)
I thank you, Director, for this conversation, and I am asking the Senate to draw the conclusions I have been expecting. They won't surprise me, although I expected them earlier.
(*Sits down on the sofa.*)

M.A. Can I put on the hat now?

KÜRMANN. I am asking you to.
(*M.A. puts on the hat and leaves.*)
I'm going to emigrate!
(*He pours himself a cup of tea.*)

DIRECTOR. Why don't you?
(*Kürmann drinks his tea.*)
Because you're waiting for Antoinette?

F.A. as Frau Hubalek brings in some mail.

KÜRMANN. Has my wife arrived yet?

F.A. No.

KÜRMANN. Thank you, Frau Hubalek, thank you.

F.A. exits.

DIRECTOR. Why don't you read your mail?
(*Kürmann reaches for the phone and dials a number.*)
Why don't you speak?

KÜRMANN. There is always this click.

DIRECTOR. You can still speak.

KÜRMANN. Why is there always this click?

DIRECTOR. Your telephone is under surveillance.
(*Kürmann hangs up the phone.*)
Some things have already changed.
(*Kürmann stands up.*)
Again, you waited the whole night long—now it's
ten in the morning, you're standing here, in your
old bathrobe, staring down at the street—

KÜRMANN. What has changed?

DIRECTOR. But you're not missing any lectures while
you're waiting for Antoinette. You were dismissed
from your professorship. And there's no whisky in
the house. In the first version, you were drinking
quite a bit while you were waiting for Antoinette.
The doctor's convinced you that your liver is at
risk, and you're feeling better than in the first
version.

Antoinette enters.

ANTOINETTE. Sorry.
(*She sits down at the breakfast table.*)
The Schneiders say hello.
(*She pours herself some tea.*)

KÜRMANN. The tea is cold.

ANTOINETTE. People were sorry that you weren't there.
I had a really good time. Some of them were very
nice, I found, very inspiring.
(*She drinks.*)
The Schneiders say hello.

KÜRMANN. You already said that.

ANTOINETTE. Did you have breakfast?

KÜRMANN. It's ten o'clock.

(*She drinks.*)

Good morning!

ANTOINETTE. Henrik says hello too.

KÜRMANN. Who?

ANTOINETTE. Henrik.

KÜRMANN. That's a surprise.

ANTOINETTE. Why is it a surprise?

KÜRMANN. Because Henrik's in London at the moment.

Antionette turns around and looks at him.

ANTOINETTE. Hannes—

KÜRMANN. Good morning!

ANTOINETTE. What's the matter?

KÜRMANN. That's what I should ask you.

ANTOINETTE. I'm coming home—

KÜRMANN. At ten in the morning.

ANTOINETTE. I said Henrik says hel—

KÜRMANN. Who's in London at the moment.

ANTOINETTE. So I'm lying?

Kürmann talks to Director—

KÜRMANN. When do I slap her?

Neon light on.

DIRECTOR. Later.

Neon light off.

KÜRMANN. Who else says hello?

F.A. as Frau Hubalek enters.

F.A. Missus Professor—

ANTOINETTE. Good morning, Frau Hubalek, good
morning.

F.A. Should I make some fresh tea?

F.A. picks up the teapot and exits.

ANTOINETTE. Have your proofs arrived?
(*She sits down and lights a cigarette.*)

DIRECTOR. She means the proofs for the paperback
you had to write to make some money: *Behavioural
Research for Dummies.*

The clock strikes ten.

KÜRMANN. Where's your watch?
(*She looks at her bare wrist.*)
I'm just asking—

Neon light on.

DIRECTOR. This is when you started yelling. First you
threw a cup, then you yelled, then you slapped her.

Neon light off.

KÜRMANN. The proofs have arrived . . .
(*He picks up his empty cup and remains standing.*)

ANTOINETTE. We've been married for two years now.
And every time I come home from a party, you
check whether or not I have my watch on. I'd like
to know what you're actually thinking!

KÜRMANN. I'm just asking.

ANTOINETTE. I already know what you're thinking!

Kürmann stirs a spoon in his empty cup.

ANTOINETTE. Every time you're thinking of some
bathroom—

(*She stands up.*)

If you want, Hannes, then I'll go. Right now. I'm not living in the nineteenth century. I won't have a man yell at me.

KÜRMANN. Did I yell at you?

(*F.A. as Frau Hubalek brings in the tea.*)

Thank you, Frau Hubalek, thank you.

F.A. exits.

ANTOINETTE. We've been married for two years now. And it is the first time I haven't come home at night, the first time, and you're making such a scene.

KÜRMANN. You're making a scene, Antoinette, not me. What am I doing? I'm listening, I'm standing and drinking tea.

ANTOINETTE. Tea?—

KÜRMANN. Tea.

ANTOINETTE. —from an empty cup!

Pause.

KÜRMANN. Why is she crying now?

DIRECTOR. That's true. In the first version, she didn't cry. Because you yelled at her, Herr Kürmann, in the first version. Now she's crying. In an argument, one partner always has to be morally superior.

ANTOINETTE. I won't tolerate this!

(*She sobs.*)

KÜRMANN. Antoinette—

(*He steps closer to her—*)

I was worried. I was working. The proofs. I called. At two in the morning. The Schneiders were already in bed. You and everyone else, so they said, had left—

Antoinette pulls something out of her purse.

ANTOINETTE. Here's my watch.
(*Kürmann goes to the table and pours himself some tea.*)
All I can say is that you're mistaken.

KÜRMANN. Well, that's fine, then.

ANTOINETTE. I don't like it at all, Hannes, I find it unacceptable! A man like you, an intellectual, a man of your age . . . I mean, a man of your experience . . .

KÜRMANN. What is it you wanted to say?

ANTOINETTE. I find it outrageous!

KÜRMANN. Really, Antoinette, now you're acting as if I'd slapped you for not coming home all night.
(*He sips the hot tea.*)
What do you find outrageous?

ANTOINETTE. We've been married for two years now—

KÜRMANN. Why didn't you call?

Antoinette puts her watch back on.

ANTOINETTE. Do you have nothing else to think about in this world? Whether or not I've slept with someone else—is that your business?
(*She takes her purse.*)
And assuming I did sleep with a man last night or every time you've imagined it—so what? Please. Would that be the end of the world?

KÜRMANN. Now you're talking nonsense.

ANTOINETTE. I did sleep with someone.

Pause.

KÜRMANN. Some more tea?

(*He pours her some tea.*)

ANTOINETTE. I need to get changed now.

KÜRMANN. Please do.

ANTOINETTE. I'm meeting someone for lunch.

(*Exit.*)

DIRECTOR. Now you know.

(*The sound of the harmonium is heard for a moment.*)
You didn't yell, Herr Kürmann, not at all. Also, the
slap didn't happen, even though Antoinette was
waiting for it. You acted like a mature man.

KÜRMANN. And what will that change?

DIRECTOR. The fact remains the same.

KÜRMANN. The fact remains the same.

DIRECTOR. But you feel better . . .

Kürmann hurls the cup to the floor.

DIRECTOR. You know what happens next?

Antoinette arrives in her coat.

ANTOINETTE. Hannes, I'll go now.

KÜRMANN. Where?

ANTOINETTE. Downtown.

KÜRMANN. Downtown.

ANTOINETTE. I told you, I have a lunch appointment.
In the afternoon, I'm in the library. As you know.
Tonight, I'll be here.

Neon light on.

DIRECTOR. Here, Herr Kürmann, you did apologize
extensively for the slap. But that's superfluous now.

Neon light off.

KÜRMANN. May I ask what his name is?

ANTOINETTE. I'd like you to leave me alone now.
That's all I can say. It's my own business. If something changes between you and me, Hannes, I'll let
you know.
(*Exit.*)

KÜRMANN. She won't say what his name is.

DIRECTOR. Even without the slap. But you do feel
better, Herr Kürmann, than in the first version.
This time, you don't have to be ashamed.
(*Kürmann cleans up the shards of the shattered cup.*)
Don't you feel better?

The harmonium and Hallelujah is heard.

KÜRMANN. Let's continue!
(*F.A. as Frau Hubalek brings in some mail.*)
Thank you, Frau Hubalek, thank you.

F.A. clears the breakfast table.

DIRECTOR. That's one week later—that's the letter for
Antoinette you opened to find out what was going
on. Remember? After that, she got herself a P.O.
box.

KÜRMANN. Frau Hubalek!
(*He gives her the letter.*)
An express letter for my wife.

F.A. takes the letter and tray and leaves.

DIRECTOR. You see, you can do better than that!
(*Kürmann drops onto the sofa.*)

Your behaviour's impeccable. Antoinette will respect you. Maybe she'll still get herself a P.O. box—not out of distrust but tact.

The harmonium is heard for a moment.

KÜRMANN. What happens in a month from now?

Neon light on.

DIRECTOR. You're still living together.
(*Neon light off.*)
Herr Kürmann, why don't you work?

Antoinette comes in wearing her coat and with a small suitcase, which she puts down to put on her gloves.

ANTOINETTE. Hannes, I'll go now.

KÜRMANN. Got everything?

ANTOINETTE. I'll be back in a week.

KÜRMANN. Got your passport?

ANTOINETTE. In a week at the latest.
(*She looks for her passport in her purse.*)

KÜRMANN. Drive carefully. I read the weather report—Gotthard Tunnel is open but Italy reports flooding.

ANTOINETTE. We're flying.

KÜRMANN. Then I'm relieved.

ANTOINETTE. Egon only gets one week off.

Pause.

KÜRMANN. When does your plane leave?

ANTOINETTE. At one o'clock I believe.
(*He looks at his watch.*)
Frau Hubalek has the household money.

KÜRMANN. I know, I gave it to her myself.

ANTOINETTE. And what are you going to do?

KÜRMANN. Proofs . . .

(She takes her small suitcase.)

You've got time, Antoinette, lots of time. It'll only take you forty minutes to the airport. At the most. And now it's ten o'clock. Not even.

(He fills his pipe.)

Why is she so nervous?

DIRECTOR. You're acting so irreproachably—Antoinette wasn't expecting that. In the first version, all this led to an endless argument. You had to admit that you opened a letter, a letter for Antoinette. She was outraged. Seven times you had to admit it and ask for forgiveness before she was capable of picking up her suitcase.

KÜRMANN. She'll be at the airport way too early now.

DIRECTOR. Because now there is nothing to forgive.

The clock strikes ten.

ANTOINETTE. Hannes, I have to go.

(She gives Kürmann a quick kiss.)

KÜRMANN. Drive safely!

(Antoinette exits.)

I mean, fly safely!

(He lights his pipe.)

His name is Egon—Egon . . .

DIRECTOR. Do you have anything against that name?

KÜRMANN. Egon!

DIRECTOR. You heard that name years ago, but never paid attention to it. People who don't know that he is Antoinette's lover, especially, them, they mention him all the time: Egon or Stahel. He's quite a pop-

ular young man, apparently, as an architect, but
also as a person—
(*Kürmann goes to the house bar.*)
There's no more whisky in the house. I told you
that earlier—you changed that, Herr Kürmann.
(*Kürmann stands, helpless.*)
Why don't you work?
(*Kürmann breaks into a fit of laughter.*)
What's so funny?

KÜRMANN. His name is Egon . . .

DIRECTOR. Herr Kürmann, *that* you can't change.

KÜRMANN. Egon . . .
(*He stops laughing.*)

DIRECTOR. If you had the chance to start over, so that
you knew exactly what you'd change in your life—
that's what you said! —but you can only change
your own actions, Herr Kürmann.
(*Neon light on.*)
In the first version, remember, there was an
encounter with Herr Stahel? You insisted on it! 'A
talk,' you said—
(*M.A. appears as Egon.*)
Would you like to change anything about that talk?
(*Kürmann looks at M.A.*)
It was, according to the dossier, a dignified talk,
even though you, Herr Kürmann, were having at
least three whiskies at the time . . .

M.A. as Egon takes a step towards Kürmann.

M.A. Hannes!

KÜRMANN. So, we're calling each other by our first
names?!

M.A. I don't know—

KÜRMANN. Take a seat, Herr Stahel.

M.A. sits down.

M.A. Or is this your armchair?

KÜRMANN. That doesn't matter.

M.A. I'm sorry!
(*He wants to get up.*)

KÜRMANN. Please!
(*M.A. remains seated, Kürmann sits down.*)
Herr Stahel, I'm grateful you accepted my invitation. We've been hearing about one another for years now, so I decided it was time to meet in person.

M.A. Thank you for your letter.

KÜRMANN. Would you like some coffee?

M.A. Not for me, no thank you

KÜRMANN. Or some tea?
(*M.A. gestures 'No.'*)
Antoinette's not home.

M.A. I know.

KÜRMANN. Does Antoinette know you're here?

M.A. I told her . . .

Pause.

KÜRMANN. Is this the first time you're in our apartment?

M.A. What do you mean?

KÜRMANN. Sometimes, I'm out of town.

M.A. Herr Kürmann—

KÜRMANN. We can talk openly.

M.A. takes out a cigarette.

M.A. It is the first time I'm in your apartment.
(*He lights the cigarette and smokes.*)

DIRECTOR. Keep going!
(*Pause.*)
Keep going!

M.A. Does it bother you if I smoke?

KÜRMANN. Not at all.

M.A. We can talk openly—

Pause.

DIRECTOR. Then why don't you?

Neon light on.

M.A. 'We've been hearing about one another for years
now—'

DIRECTOR. We know that already.

M.A. 'I've got nothing to blame you for. We love the
same woman. I understand you. A woman isn't one
man's property, after all. I don't think we need to
teach that to one another. And Antoinette loves
you. That's the way it is. As far as I am concerned,
I've got nothing to blame you for.'

DIRECTOR. Which of you says that?

M.A. Herr Kürmann.

DIRECTOR. And what does the other one say?

M.A. 'Egon smiles.'
(*He smiles.*)

KÜRMANN. Perhaps it's ridiculous—I know—there's
really nothing to discuss. On the other hand, I
thought it just as ridiculous that we should never
meet at all. Why not? We live in the same city—

M.A. That's true.

KÜRMANN. And we love the same woman—
(*M.A. stands up.*)
Or is that not true?

M.A. (*takes the ashtray from the desk*). May I?
(*He sits down again.*)
We love the same woman, Herr Kürmann, I know, Herr Kürmann, for years. We both know that. And hardly a week passes without me hearing your name—Hannes is losing his professorship, Hannes and his gastritis, Hannes is travelling to the Soviet Union—

KÜRMANN. I hear rather little about you.

M.A. Even I thought it was time that—

KÜRMANN. You're an architect and a Catholic.

M.A. You could say so, I guess.

KÜRMANN. And married as well.

M.A. Let's keep my wife out of this.

KÜRMANN. She doesn't know about Antoinette?

M.A. Even I thought it was time that—you're totally right. We live in the same city—why shouldn't we meet, after all, and get to know each other in person? Why not? For a long time, I've been feeling the need for an honest talk, man to man, even if that won't change anything.

KÜRMANN. And yet you never called.

M.A. I've been wanting to write.

KÜRMANN. What prevented you?

M.A. You know Antoinette.

KÜRMANN. What do you mean?

M.A. You're married to her—

KÜRMANN. Which doesn't mean I know her.

M.A. You've no idea how many times I asked your wife, Hannes, to tell you about our relationship. It's an important relationship to me, believe me. I've begged. She couldn't, she said. I've been insisting that you, her husband, be informed, at least since you and Antoinette got married.

KÜRMANN. Since we got married . . .

M.A. I've been insisting, but Antoinette didn't want me to tell you either. Then everything would be over. Between us. She couldn't hurt a person she appreciates that much.

KÜRMANN. Since we got married . . .

M.A. Antoinette appreciates you.

KÜRMANN. But she did tell me.

M.A. Only after I had threatened to write to you—my letter was already on the desk—and after I put Antoinette on the spot. 'You either talk to Hannes—today!—or I'll send my letter.' A registered letter.

KÜRMANN. When was that?

M.A. I couldn't bear it any longer!

KÜRMANN. I believe you, Egon.

M.A. That was a year and a half ago, I think. It was very hard for Antoinette, but I insisted. Afterwards, Antoinette was so relieved. An end to all this lying! Back then, it felt like I was relieved of a burden. Our relationship got happier too.

KÜRMANN. A year and a half ago—

M.A. Much happier.

KÜRMANN. She told me a month ago.

Pause.

DIRECTOR. Continue, gentlemen, continue!

M.A. stands up, puts his hands in his pockets and looks out the window.

KÜRMANN. Unfortunately, I've no whisky in the house.

M.A. I understand!

KÜRMANN. I stopped drinking.

M.A. —that's why she didn't want me, under any circumstances, to meet you today. That's why! She told me a year and a half ago, 'Now Hannes knew everything.'
(*He laughs—*)
We love the same woman, God knows, yeah.

Pause.

DIRECTOR. Go on, gentlemen, go on!

Kürmann goes across to Director—

KÜRMANN. I abstain from this talk.

DIRECTOR. As you wish.

KÜRMANN. It doesn't work without the whisky.

Neon light on.

DIRECTOR. Herr Kürmann abstains from this talk.
(*M.A. exits.*)
So that means—
(*Flips through the dossier—*)
—you'll never meet Herr Stahel. You won't know how much he suffered since you and Antoinette got married. And it won't end in a friendship with Egon.

KÜRMANN. It doesn't work without the whisky.

DIRECTOR. So that's cut, then.

(*He pulls out some pages from the book and throws them aside.*)

Please.

Neon light off. Kürmann sits down at the desk.

KÜRMANN. Frau Hubalek?

(*The harmonium is heard.*)

Frau Hubalek!

DIRECTOR. Why are you shouting?

F.A. enters as an Italian woman.

F.A. *Professore—*?

DIRECTOR. Frau Hubalek is dead.

F.A. *Che cosa desidere?*

KÜRMANN. What's ashtray?

DIRECTOR. *Portacenere.*

KÜRMANN. *Per favore.*

DIRECTOR. Her name is Pina and she's from Calabria.

KÜRMANN. *Come sta*, Pina?

F.A. *Meglioi, Signore, un po meglio.*

(*She takes away the full ashtray.*)

KÜRMANN. *Brutto tempo in questo paese.*

F.A. Eh!

KÜRMANN. Eh!

F.A. exits.

DIRECTOR. Your Italian's getting better.

KÜRMANN. Is there anyone else who's dead?

DIRECTOR. Not in this house.

F.A. brings in the clean ashtray.

KÜRMANN. *Grazie,* Nina.

DIRECTOR. Pina!

KÜRMANN. Pina, *mille grazie!*
(*F.A. exits.*)
What else has happened?

Antoinette comes in wearing a new coat.

ANTOINETTE. Hannes, I'm going now.

DIRECTOR. She bought a new coat.

KÜRMANN. In the afternoon, you're in the library.

ANTOINETTE. In the afternoon, I'm in the library.

KÜRMANN. In the evening, you'll be here.

ANTOINETTE. I don't know yet.
(*She gives him a quick kiss.*)

KÜRMANN. She doesn't know yet!

Antoinette turns to leave.

KÜRMANN. Stop!
(*Antoinette stops.*)
That's what I want to change.

DIRECTOR. Please.

KÜRMANN. Once and for all.

DIRECTOR. Herr Kürmann wants to change something.

ANTOINETTE. Please.
(*She comes back in.*)
Hannes, I'm going now.

KÜRMANN. Why don't we get a divorce?

ANTOINETTE. In the afternoon, I'm in the library.

KÜRMANN. I asked you something.

ANTOINETTE. In the evening, I'll be here.

KÜRMANN. Why don't we get a divorce!

Pause.

DIRECTOR. In the first version, this morning, you gave
her the following reason—

Kürmann sits down on the edge of his desk.

F.A. 'It's a waste of our time, Antoinette. I love you,
Antoinette, but it's a waste of our time.'

Pause.

KÜRMANN. A waste of time . . .
(*He steps towards the window and looks out.*)

F.A. 'We only live once, Antoinette.'

KÜRMANN. That's what I said?

DIRECTOR. Trivial, yes, but genuine!

Kürmann sits at his desk again.

F.A. 'Once, years ago, remember, you said, "If something changes between you and me, Hannes, I'll let
you know."'

Antoinette is silent.

KÜRMANN. Remember?

DIRECTOR. We remember.

KÜRMANN. And yet, nothing will change. Egon is
Catholic. He cannot get a divorce. That sanctifies
our own marriage too.
(*Antoinette is silent.*)
I know you don't like being talked to in this tone.
However, I'm urging you to get a divorce.
(*Antoinette is silent.*)
As soon as possible!
(*Antoinette is silent.*)
Did you hear me?

Antoinette sits down.

ANTOINETTE. Have you talked to a lawyer.

KÜRMANN. No.

ANTOINETTE. I have—
(*She lights a cigarette.*)
It would make it easier if we had the same one, says
my lawyer. If it comes down to a litigation, it could
take at least a year—and, he says, it would also get
more expensive for you.

Kürmann goes to Director's desk.

KÜRMANN. What happens in a year?
(*The sound of a baby crying.*)
A baby?

DIRECTOR. Yes.

KÜRMANN. With Egon?

DIRECTOR. No.

KÜRMANN. With me?

DIRECTOR. The young Calabrian woman had a baby.

The baby is silent.

KÜRMANN. What else?

DIRECTOR. You've been to Moscow.

KÜRMANN. And?

DIRECTOR. You don't talk about it. Certain people
believe your silence to be evidence of the fact that
you were disappointed with the Soviet Union.

ANTOINETTE. Which is the truth.

KÜRMANN. How do you know?

ANTOINETTE. Egon has also been to Russia,

KÜRMANN. Egon!

ANTOINETTE. He reported to me.

KÜRMANN. Egon is a reactionary.

Antoinette puts out her cigarette.

ANTOINETTE. Hannes, I'm going now.

KÜRMANN. How are things between us, a year later?

DIRECTOR. You still want a divorce . . .

Antoinette looks at her watch.

ANTOINETTE. There's nothing we haven't already told
one another. Either we'll finally see a lawyer, or
we'll never talk about a divorce ever again.
(*She gets up.*)
In the afternoon, I'm in the library.

KÜRMANN. In the afternoon, she's in the library—

ANTOINETTE. In the evening, I'll be here.

KÜRMANN. In the evening, she'll be here—

ANTOINETTE. Or I'll call.

KÜRMANN. Or she'll call . . .

*Kürmann steps into the scene, opens a desk drawer,
takes a gun out and looks at it, deep in thought.*

DIRECTOR. You've been there before.
(*Neon light on.*)
You wanted to shoot yourself because you thought,
you loved this woman and nothing could be done
about it—
(*Kürmann cocks the gun.*)
The gun's loaded, Herr Kürmann.
(*Kürmann stares into space.*)
To be honest, we expected something different,
something more bold—

KÜRMANN. Yeah.

DIRECTOR. —nothing spectacular perhaps, but something different, something you haven't already lived. At the very least, something different. Why, for example, didn't you emigrate?—since you had the choice again . . . Instead, the same apartment, the same story with Antoinette. Except the slap. That you changed. And what else? You're not drinking. That's all you changed, and that's what this spectacle was for?!

KÜRMANN. I love her.

Neon light off.

DIRECTOR. As you please.

Antoinette enters in her coat.

ANTOINETTE. Hannes, I'm going now.
(*Kürmann points the gun at her.*)
Downtown.
(*A gun shot.*)
In the afternoon, I'm in the library.
(*Gun shot.*)
In the evening, I'll be here.
(*Gun shot.*)
Hannes—

KÜRMANN. She thinks I'm dreaming this.

A shot.

ANTOINETTE. Don't you hear what I'm saying?

A shot. Antoinette breaks down.

DIRECTOR. Yes, Herr Kürmann, *now* you've shot!

KÜRMANN. I did?

(*Antoinette lies motionless on the floor. Director goes to her and kneels down beside her, while Kürmann can*

only stand there, paralysed, watching. M.A. and F.A.
take care of Antoinette.)
No! No—

DIRECTOR. You fired five shots at your wife, Antoinette
Kürmann, née Stein, Ph.D. The fifth shot, to the
head, was fatal . . . During the investigation, you
said that you were surprised, you never thought you
were capable of doing that—
(*Kürmann is silent.*)
May I now ask you a question?
(*Pause.*)
Do you now think, with regard to this biography,
or, better still, do you now believe—now feel, now
that you're living in this cell, a—how can I put it—
a tendency, an urge, a disposition which you never
knew before and which has only evolved out of an
awareness of your guilt, a—disposition—to repent?

KÜRMANN. To what?

DIRECTOR. You are forty-nine now, Herr Kürmann. A
penalty reduction—which is, as we know, not
impossible in case of good behaviour—should not
be expected before twelve years are served. You will
then be sixty-one, assuming you live that long . . .
You understand?

KÜRMANN. You mean, in order to bear such a prospect,
I'd better start looking for a reason, for some meaning, in what happened?

DIRECTOR. I'm asking.

KÜRMANN. And this meaning would have to consist of
my belief that this is how it had to happen—no
other way? Which we can't prove but believe. Like
this and no other way. Destiny. Providence.

DIRECTOR. We could say so.

KÜRMANN. I know how it happened.

DIRECTOR. By accident?

KÜRMANN. It didn't have to.

Pause.

DIRECTOR. Herr Kürmann, the choice is yours.

KÜRMANN. To believe or not to believe.

DIRECTOR. Yes.

Kürmann is silent.

KÜRMANN. And she?—Antoinette? . . . Whether or not I believe it, what is this going to change for her? Her life—not my life . . . What does it do for the dead that I, a murderer, should decorate my cell with destiny? I destroyed a life—her life. What is choice supposed to be here? She is dead—dead— and I am choosing—to believe or not to believe! Repentance! Whatever you mean by repentance—

DIRECTOR. What are you trying to say?

KÜRMANN. Antoinette could be alive . . . It didn't have to be . . . Living—eating—laughing—dreaming of her gallery that will never exist—having somebody's baby—telling lies—sleeping—wearing a new dress—living . . .

DIRECTOR. Then let's go back again.

KÜRMANN. Please.

DIRECTOR. The choice is yours, Herr Kürmann.

KÜRMANN. No gun.

DIRECTOR. No shooting this time.

Antoinette gets up from the floor.

ANTOINETTE. Thanks.

DIRECTOR. No gun. As you wish.

KÜRMANN. Thanks.

Stage light on the room: a small group of party guests slightly dishevelled and perhaps about to leave.

M.A. Where is Kürmann? We have to tell him— Antoinette is a genius. Kürmann!

F.A. Don't shout.

ANTOINETTE. I haven't played the spinet for years.

M.A. We have to tell him—Antoinette is a genius.— What's with the garden gnomes?

ANTOINETTE. Should I make a flour soup?

M.A. I've been hearing this question for an hour now . . .

Silence.

F.A. *Un ange passes . . .*

M.A. (*calling outside*). Schneider, do you want flour soup?

F.A. What's with the garden gnomes?

ANTOINETTE. Who wants some flour soup?

F.A. Garden gnomes. Antoinette!
(*Trying to whisper something in her ear.*)

M.A. No whispering ! So, what about the flour soup then?

KÜRMANN. I'll make the flour soup.

M.A. Kürmann has been resurrected. Your wife is fabulous, just so you know, Kürmann! You don't deserve such a wife at all!

KÜRMANN. But that'll take a little while.

M.A. You don't deserve such a husband at all, Antoinette, just so you know! You both don't deserve one another at all!

F.A. (*leaving*). Antoinette must go on playing.

M.A. (*leaving*). Muggy, why aren't *you* a genius?

F.A. Don't always shout.
(*From outside—*)
Guys, we should go.

Kürmann enters.

DIRECTOR. I thought you were making flour soup. What's the matter? Aren't you feeling well? Your friends are waiting for the flour soup.

KÜRMANN. What happens in a year from now?

DIRECTOR. You want to know?

KÜRMANN. What happens in a year from now?

Work lights.

DIRECTOR. Antoinette has gone downtown. It is eleven in the morning, Herr Kürmann, and you're still in your bathrobe.
(*Kürmann sits down at his desk.*)
You're thinking too much about Antoinette—

A baby's crying can be heard.

KÜRMANN. Pina? Where is she?

DIRECTOR. Shopping perhaps.

KÜRMANN. Pina!

The baby is quiet.

DIRECTOR. May I sit?
(*He sits. Kürmann doesn't look up.*)

You're despairing. . . . Millions of your contemporaries have harder lives than Hannes Kürmann—you're aware of that. Yet you're despairing. I understand. What do you do with your freedom? You changed little things here and there. Hannes Kürmann no longer drinks alcohol. Bravo! He made up his mind to get a divorce, but it takes two people to go through with it. Yet he remains determined to get a divorce. Bravo! And? Hannes Kürmann is no longer part of what is called the faculty body. Bravo! You chose independence—

KÜRMANN. Stop it!

DIRECTOR. In half a year you're turning fifty.

(*Kürmann looks up.*)

You're in despair about yourself.

Kürmann laughs.

KÜRMANN. Should I start doing yoga?

(*He stands up. Director remains seated.*)

DIRECTOR. There are many different doctrines . . .

KÜRMANN. The sum of all banalities remains the same.

DIRECTOR. Sounds like a formula.

KÜRMANN. It's the truth.

The baby's crying is heard again.

DIRECTOR. Well.

(*The baby is quiet.*)

You were going to say something?

(*A harmonium is heard.*)

Well.

(*The harmonium is quiet.*)

I understand you! You had the choice to alter your biography, that's what we all desire sometimes, and the outcome—variations of the banal.

KÜRMANN (*yells*). What should I do?!

The baby cries.

DIRECTOR. Well.
(*The baby is quiet.*)
Why not yoga?

KÜRMANN. Yoga . . .

DIRECTOR. Yoga à l'Americaine, now practised by a lot of people who suffer from a banal biography.
(*He stands up.*)
Try it!

KÜRMANN. Yoga . . .

DIRECTOR. Why not?
(*He looks at his watch.*)
You don't have much time left.
(*Goes back to his desk.*)

Kürmann is standing alone.

VOICE OFFSTAGE. Feel how your body is breathing.
Your body.
How it is breathing.
Without your will.
Feel this breathing through your whole body and nothing but this breathing without your will.
Can you feel it?

KÜRMANN. Yes.

VOICE OFFSTAGE. And nothing but this breathing.

KÜRMANN. Oh yes.

VOICE OFFSTAGE. Don't force yourself.

Feel how your body stands.
Without your will.
How it breathes and stands.
Your body.
Think of nothing else.
That's important.
Can you feel yourself?

KÜRMANN. Yes—

VOICE OFFSTAGE. Relax all of your muscles.
Try it.
All of them.
It's not easy at first, I know. Until you begin to
trust that your body won't fall once you relax your
muscles, and you no longer have control over your
thoughts.
Your body.
Feel nothing else.
Try it.
*Stage light in front of the room scene: in its white pool
appears F.A. as a nurse and with a wheelchair.*

F.A. You mustn't get up yet, Herr Kürmann, two
weeks after the surgery, you need to be patient,
Herr Kürmann, patient.
(*She leads Kürmann to the wheelchair.*)
The doctor will be here in just a minute.
(*She exits.*)

KÜRMANN. Is it the liver?

DIRECTOR. Apparently not.

KÜRMANN. Then what?

DIRECTOR. You did take better care of your liver,
after all.

KÜRMANN. Why an operation?

F.A. brings in flowers.

F.A. See, Herr Kürmann, see—flowers from your son in America, all this delphinium, so much delphinium!

KÜRMANN. Nurse—?

F.A. Agnes.

KÜRMANN. May I talk to the head physician?

F.A. arranges the flowers in a vase.

F.A. Just a minute, Herr Kürmann, just a minute. (*Exits.*)

DIRECTOR. Are you in pain?

KÜRMANN. Not at the moment.

DIRECTOR. That's the morphine.
(*M.A. enters as a gentleman with a black monocle.*)
Do you want visitors?

M.A. Hannes—

DIRECTOR. Snotler. Remember the snowball fight? He made his way in the world, you see, even without his left eye. He's a sales manager. He wants to talk about South Africa.
(*Kürmann turns his head away.*)
He doesn't want any visitors today.

M.A. exits.

KÜRMANN. How long have I been in this clinic?

DIRECTOR. Since February.

KÜRMANN. It's May now?

DIRECTOR. June.

KÜRMANN. Do they know what it is?

DIRECTOR. The head physician says, 'Gastritis.'

KÜRMANN. What's that?

DIRECTOR. A protracted gastritis . . .

Director picks up a chair from beside his desk and puts it down in the pool of light beside the wheelchair where Kürmann sits.

KÜRMANN. Today, I wanted to go into the garden—

DIRECTOR. I understand.

KÜRMANN. Summer is coming.

DIRECTOR. The delphiniums are out, yes.

KÜRMANN. When will I be home again?

DIRECTOR. You need to ask the head physician that—
(*Goes back to the his desk.*)
Could we turn the stage light up a bit, please?
(*It gets darker.*)
Up!
(*It gets brighter.*)
Or would you prefer the curtains closed when the sun is shining, like it is today, Herr Kürmann?
(*Kürmann shakes his head.*)
All right.

M.A. as Egon sits on the chair.

M.A. A warm day—
(*He loosens his tie and collar.*)

DIRECTOR. You remember, Herr Kürmann—an earlier encounter—'a talk'? You abstained from it in the new version, which means this is your first conversation with Egon Stahel.

KÜRMANN. Why don't you take off your jacket?

M.A. It's much cooler inside . . .

(*Pause.*)

I haven't seen Antoinette for a year. No, I didn't hear from her that you were in this clinic . . . It shocked me quite a bit, Hannes . . . I don't even know who told me.

(*He takes out a cigarette.*)

How is Antoinette?

(*He takes out his lighter.*)

We no longer write to each other.

KÜRMANN. For a year?

M.A. I thought you knew.

KÜRMANN. Antoinette keeps very much to herself.

(*Pause.*)

Do you really not want to take off your jacket?

M.A. lights his cigarette.

M.A. I think it was Lore who told me.

KÜRMANN. Who is Lore?

M.A. My wife.

KÜRMANN. What did she say?

M.A. That you have stomach cancer.

(*Pause.*)

Therefore I was glad, to be honest, that you had abstained from our talk. Back then. What could we have told one another?! Two men who love the same woman . . . Does it bother you, Hannes, if I smoke?

KÜRMANN. There's no ashtray in here.

M.A. I don't have to anyway.

(*He steps on the cigarette to put it out.*)

She never told me much about you and yet, as the years went by, I felt I knew you, Hannes, better

than my other friends. . . . Yes . . . Secretly, I talked
to you often, Hannes, more openly than with
Antoinette.
(*He puts a new cigarette in his mouth.*)
She's an unhappy woman.

KÜRMANN. Why?

M.A. At first, I thought it was because of you . . .

F.A. as nurse appears with a medication cart.

F.A. Smoking's not allowed in here.

M.A. I'm sorry.

F.A. The doctor will be here in a minute.
(*She exits.*)

M.A. Are you in pain?

KÜRMANN. Yes.

M.A. I'll go now. . . . Actually, I didn't want to talk
about Antoinette . . . You do love her, after all, I
know.
(*He stands up.*)
I know Professor Fink. I built his country home. A
good doctor, they say.

KÜRMANN. I went to see him years ago.

Pause.

M.A. Hannes, I will miss you.
(*He extends his hand.*)

KÜRMANN. What are you trying to say?

M.A. You know.

KÜRMANN. You're the only one who's being honest
with me.
(*A knocking at the door.*)
Thank you, Egon.

(*Knocking again.*)
Come in!

Antoinette enters in her coat and with a bag.

ANTOINETTE. Ah.
(*A silent greeting, then M.A. exits.*)
I got you the books.
(*She takes some books out of her bag.*)

KÜRMANN. Egon was here.

ANTOINETTE. We just ran into each other.

KÜRMANN. Did you—?

Antoinette sits beside him.

ANTOINETTE. Are you in pain?

KÜRMANN. They're going to give me an injection.

Antoinette takes his hand.

KÜRMANN. Today, I wanted to go into the garden—

M.A. comes in, in a white coat.

M.A. Well, Herr Kürmann, how are you doing?
(*Antoinette gets up.*)
Herr Kürmann wants to walk!

ANTOINETTE. So I've just heard.

M.A. How did you sleep last night?
(*He feels Kürmann's pulse.*)

KÜRMANN. Doctor—

M.A. Your pulse is better already.

KÜRMANN. Can I talk to you alone?

M.A. Herr Kürmann, we need to be patient. The tiredness, as you know, is a result of the radiation—it doesn't mean anything.

ANTOINETTE. I'll wait outside.

(*She goes away.*)

M.A. Your pulse is better, much better.

KÜRMANN. Do they know now what it is?

M.A. Gastritis.
(*He takes off his glasses to clean them.*)
A particularly tedious gastritis.
(*He holds the glasses up against the light.*)
I know, Herr Kürmann, I know what you're think-
ing, what everybody's thinking nowadays when
they hear 'radiation'.
(*He puts his glasses back on.*)
You're thinking too much.

KÜRMANN. I want you to be honest with me.

M.A. We need to be patient.

KÜRMANN. Does gastritis get treated with surgery?

M.A. You didn't have surgery, Herr Kürmann.

KÜRMANN. Then why did they tell me—

M.A. Who did?

KÜRMANN. Nurse Agnes.

M.A. takes a book from the chair.

M.A. What are you reading, by the way?
(*He flips through the pages, without reading.*)
Of course, we thought of it too, otherwise we
wouldn't have considered the operation. I don't
want to conceal that from you. Radiation is not
very pleasant—we know that. But as long as you're
staying here, I mean until we know that this gastritis won't come back—you've probably had a gastritis before, stomach-aches, but you thought it was
the liver.

KÜRMANN. That was the diagnosis back then.

M.A. reads the title on the book cover.

M.A. *Italian for Beginners.*
(*He puts the book down.*)
You want to know when you'll be able to travel, I understand that, Herr Kürmann, I understand that—

KÜRMANN. We'd like to go to Tuscany.

M.A. Tuscany is still nice in the fall.
(*Kürmann is silent.*)
As I said, Herr Kürmann—

KÜRMANN. Is it cancer?

M.A. A certain risk exists, of course, at our age—that's what the statistics show. In any case, it would be irresponsible if we didn't do radiation.

KÜRMANN. I'm just scared.

M.A. Of the radiation?

KÜRMANN. Of dying slowly . . .

Pause.

M.A. What lovely flowers you've got today!

KÜRMANN. Yes.

M.A. Herr Kürmann—
(*He offers his hand.*)

KÜRMANN. Does my wife know?

M.A. Until tomorrow, Herr Kürmann, I will see you tomorrow.
(*He exits.*)

Antoinette comes back in.

KÜRMANN. Tuscany, he said, is still nice in the fall . . .

Antoinette picks up the book and sits.

ANTOINETTE. Where were we?

KÜRMANN. *Decima Lezione.*

ANTOINETTE. What would you like, sir?

KÜRMANN. *Che cosa desidera, Signore?*

ANTOINETTE. *Signora desidera.*

KÜRMANN. *Vorrei una cravatta.*

ANTOINETTE. Where is the mirror?

KÜRMANN. *Dove si trova il specchio?*

ANTOINETTE. *Lo specchio.*

KÜRMANN. *Lo specchio, lo studio, lo spazio.*

ANTOINETTE. *Plurale?*

KÜRMANN. *Gli specchi.*

ANTOINETTE. Lesson Eleven.

KÜRMANN. I've been meaning to write to you. Every time you're here, they give me an injection and I don't remember what I wanted to write.

Neon light on.

DIRECTOR. 'Antoinette, we have reduced one another. Why did we always reduce one another? I did it to you, you to me. Why did we reduce everything of all that was possible? We only know each other reduced like this.'

Neon light off.

ANTOINETTE. Lesson Eleven.

KÜRMANN. *Undicesima lezione.*

F.A. as nurse comes in.

F.A. Herr Kürmann—

KÜRMANN. Here comes the injection again.

F.A. You'll feel better in a moment.

(*She gives him an injection.*)
Herr Kürmann will feel better in a moment.
(*She touches the wound up.*)
Keep the cotton pressed down on it.
(*She pushes the medication cart out.*)

KÜRMANN. You've been to Tuscany?

ANTOINETTE. Yes, Hannes, yes.

KÜRMANN. I haven't.
(*F.A. as the nurse comes back in.*)
They want to do radiation again.

F.A. pushes Kürmann out in his wheelchair.

ANTOINETTE. I'll come back in the afternoon!
(*She looks towards Director.*)
Do you think he knows?

DIRECTOR. At times.
(*Antoinette starts sobbing.*)
It can take months, and you're coming every day,
now twice a day. You can't save him either, Frau
Kürmann, you know that.

ANTOINETTE. Yes.

DIRECTOR. In a few years from now, who knows,
maybe there'll be a cure, but for now it's still fate.
(*Antoinette turns to leave.*)
Frau Kürmann!
(*He steps closer to her.*)
Do you regret your time with Hannes?
(*Antoinette stares at Director.*)
You too have the choice again, of course, you too
can start over—if you know what you'd like to do
different in your life.

ANTOINETTE. And how well I know that!

DIRECTOR. Where would you like to begin?

ANTOINETTE. Seven years ago. At two in the morning.

DIRECTOR. Then please, Miss Stein. Please.

(Stage light off.)
(Work lights.)
Back again!

M.A. Do we need the musical clock again?

DIRECTOR. Of course.

(M.A. brings the musical clock.)
Are the ashtrays there?

M.A. Yes.

(He exits.)

DIRECTOR. We are ready.

(Stage lighting.)
Miss Stein?

Antoinette enters in her evening dress, sits down on the fauteuil and waits. She is wearing the dark horn-rimmed glasses. Laughter, then silence. Shortly after, Kürmann appears, dressed as at the beginning of the game. He stands, helpless.

ANTOINETTE. I'll be leaving soon, too.

DIRECTOR. Are you feeling unwell?

ANTOINETTE. On the contrary.

(She takes a cigarette.)
Just one more cigarette.
(She waits in vain for a lighter.)
If I'm not bothering you.
(She lights it and smokes.)
I had a really good time. Some of them were very nice, I found, very inspiring . . .

The clock strikes two.

KÜRMANN. It's two o'clock.

ANTOINETTE. You are tired.

KÜRMANN. I have to work tomorrow.

ANTOINETTE. What do you do?

(*Pause.*)

Actually, I just wanted to hear your old musical clock again. Musical clocks have always fascinated me—these figures that always make the same gestures every time it goes off—

(*Kürmann goes to the musical clock and winds it, a cheerful jingle is heard, he turns the barrel until the song is finished.*)

I'm leaving now.

KÜRMANN. Do you have a car?

ANTOINETTE. Yes.

(*She stands up and picks up her jacket.*)

Why are you looking at me like that?

(*He helps her put on her jacket.*)

Why are you looking at me like that?

(*She takes her purse.*)

I have to work tomorrow.

She is ready, Kürmann brings her to the door and comes back into the room immediately.

KÜRMANN. And now?

DIRECTOR. She is gone.

KÜRMANN. And now?

DIRECTOR. Now you are free.

KÜRMANN. Free—

DIRECTOR. A biography without Antoinette.

Neon light on.

M.A. 'After the guests had left, she just sat there. What do you do with a strange lady who won't leave, who just stays and sits there in silence at two o'clock in the morning? It didn't have to be that way . . .'

Neon light off.

DIRECTOR. You are free, Kürmann—for another seven years.

Curtain.